G000109555

The Break-up Survival Kit

The Break-up Survival Kit

Emotional Rescue for the Newly Single

DR PAM SPURR

 ROBSON BOOKS

For Sam and Stephie – two shining lights.
For Nilk – an incredible husband. And for my mother and late
father – you gave me hope.

First published in Great Britain in 2001 by Robson Books
10 Blenheim Court, Brewery Road, London N7 9NT

A member of the Chrysalis Group plc

Copyright © 2001 Pam Spurr

The right of Pam Spurr to be identified as the author of this work
has been asserted by her in accordance with the Copyright,
Designs and Patents Act 1988

Nutritional advice supplied by Dr Doug Spurr

British Library Cataloguing in Publication Data
A catalogue record for this title is available from the British Library

ISBN 1 86105 384 3

All rights reserved. No part of this publication may be reproduced,
stored in a retrieval system, or transmitted in any form or by any
means, electronic, mechanical, photocopying, recording or
otherwise, without the prior permission in writing of the
publishers.

Typeset by SX Composing DTP, Rayleigh, Essex
Printed in Great Britain by
Creative Print & Design (Wales), Ebbw Vale

CONTENTS

Acknowledgements   vi

Introduction   1

1   Facing Reality   9

2   Smoke Signals   27

3   The Chameleon Factor   39

4   Sex and the Newly Single   55

5   Getting Even   69

6   The Divorce Diet   77

7   How Hung Up Are You On Your Ex?   101

8   Me? I Used to Love Him/Her?   111

Acknowledgements

I'd like to thank the men and women who've shared their break-up pain with me and who found their own solutions to moving on. This book is for anyone surviving the pain of break-up – straight, gay, bisexual or transgendered.

Lorna Russell has been a tremendous help in ensuring THE BREAK-UP SURVIVAL KIT retained a positive message and an upbeat tone. Others may not have so clearly understood the essence of the message I hope to convey. Finally Jeremy Robson, Andrea Molley and John Allgrove were so positive about getting behind this book that it helped and encouraged me in the task of writing it.

INTRODUCTION

This book is called *The Break-Up Survival Kit* as after a relationship break-up it often becomes a case of how do I survive? 'This feels so awful – how can I cope?' people ask. They fear that they quite simply won't survive! Then their entire lives get bound up with their reactions to the break-up. Their friendships, their work life, their sleep patterns, their drinking and even their eating habits change. (Think of the people you've barely recognised after a break-up because they've shrunk down to nothing due to the emotional stress or because they want to prove a point to their ex.) Although this book tackles all these areas it is less about 'salad' and more about the emotional junk food that gets stuck in our hearts and minds after a break-up. Let's begin by getting a few things straight as we've got work to do!

The Break-Up Survival Kit is for anyone who has suffered a break-up. This means any relationship break-up – whether you two were married, co-habiting, or simply dating, whether recent or past, fair or unfair, seemingly trouble-free or fraught with difficulties, dumper or dumpee.

Yes, I include the *dumpers* among you because they may go through break-up pain too. You may ask how they get hurt – when they're the ones who've said 'bye-bye' and 'no more'. Well, why do you think many of them dumped in the first place? Did they dump because they were happy? No, that would be crazy. Did they dump because the relationship fulfilled them? No, because that would be silly. More than likely they dumped because they were in emotional pain, too. They were depressed, desolate and desperate. The three

Ds of break-up. Of course, there will be those few individuals who dump partners because they get some sort of sadistic kick out of hurting others but we're not including them here. They deserve their own book – *How to Recognise a Romantic Psycho.*

I know for a fact, from personal and professional experience, that dumpers are frequently confused and unhappy. As I will be recounting the case studies of many others throughout *The Break-Up Survival Kit,* I'll explain this point from a personal perspective first. I didn't divorce my husband of 10 years in 1992 because I was happy! I was miserable; I was emotionally drained; I was depressed, desolate and desperate. The marriage I had so wanted to last 'for ever' was crushing me as a lover, a person and a mother. And when it finally dawned on me that it was even affecting my ability to be the best possible mother to the two dearest people in my life – my son and daughter – I then knew it was time to dump. So not a happy dumping story – a desperately sad one.

In fact, I've heard so many sad stories, and so much about sad, mad, and bad behaviour over the years that I've pulled together some information to hammer home the point about how many 'walking wounded' are out there suffering and in many ways. Marital and relationship breakdown is rife in our society. The UK now has a divorce rate almost matching that of the USA, with 40% of marriages ending in divorce. For example, in 1998 approximately 160,000 divorces were granted in Britain compared with 80,000 in 1971. That's approximately 320,000 people in varying degrees of pain.

The emotional 'fall-out' from the trauma of divorce is incalculable. Psychological, social, and medical research shows that this ranks as one of the top negative life events impacting on the individual's entire sense of emotional and physical well-being. Further findings conclude that marital breakdown leads to higher rates of depression, anxiety, lowered self-esteem, general stress and medical problems like increased risk of infections, lowered immune system response, high blood pressure and gastro-intestinal problems. Relationship breakdown among those who co-habit is even more frequent. Although less well documented, I think we can make an educated guess that much emotional and physical suffering takes place in this group. Just because they didn't commit to the wedding day doesn't mean that they didn't escape heartbreak.

Now, aside from all the health problems associated with relationship breakdown, what else do people in pain do? They tend to make very bad decisions. During the break-up their sense of judgement goes out the window with their self-esteem. This is the time when someone you've known for ages suddenly does something out of character. You know the sort of thing I mean – when a friend who's always been steady and reliable becomes completely disorganised. And that's just the start of it. She also decides it's a good idea to have an affair with her boss. You watch helplessly as it all ends in tears because she simply won't listen to what you have to say. Or you watch as another friend starts 'comfort bingeing' as soon as she hears, sees, or even imagines any news about the ex that dumped her. Remember – people in the middle of pain have the most amazing capacity to let their imaginations run wild about their ex. They imagine that their ex has become the most popular person on the planet, that their ex is invited to constant parties and events, that their ex is having the time of their life while they wallow in misery.

This is a time when people are absolutely driven by their demons. Sometimes they're determined to prove something to themselves, their ex, or even their family – particularly if family members take a 'told-you-so' attitude towards their ex – giving all those knowing looks that say 'I knew it would end in tears.' Sometimes they're driven to try to revenge themselves on their ex – something we'll discuss in detail in Chapter Five. At other times, even they can't fathom out the reason for their troublesome behaviour. Dark, angry, hurt, sad and sorry emotions drive them like a whirlwind. However, it all boils down to one thing – that they've wasted this enormous energy by doing things that are emotionally destructive and negative. *The Break-Up Survival Kit* is all about turning around this energy to do something positive and constructive for yourself. It is coming to your own emotional rescue, to help you enjoy life again.

Of course, sometimes we have to go through even more bad times (the original 'badness' being the break-up) before realising that there is *another* way, that there are options to our crazy behaviour. Julie is an example of someone who had to take one step too far before realising that she didn't have to waste her time and energy. Julie's ex, Nick, had committed the worst sin – he'd dumped her for someone younger after six years of marriage. So, not only did she feel utterly betrayed by his adultery but she had to cope with the double whammy of the 'new model' being younger and prettier. Julie's self-esteem dived to previously unplumbed depths.

How did Julie respond? Did she lick her wounds, seek solace in her friends, and get a new hobby? Did she buy one of those padded voodoo dolls, put a few pins in it and hope her ex got a serious case of impotency? (Not the most pleasant of images but at least she wouldn't really be hurting anyone.) No, she took up with the office junior who happened to be her boss's son. Pretty silly, don't you think? Well, she didn't think so. In Julie's mind she wanted to demonstrate that she could attract someone younger, too.

Where did this madness end? After doing a 'Mrs Robinson' and seducing the young man, who was ten years younger than her, it spread around the office like wildfire. Her young love soon lost interest in the novelty and decided that he didn't want to see her any more. As the gossip grew so too did the risk that her boss would find out. Julie felt sick each day as she approached work – sick for fear of being hauled before the boss and sick with dejection that her young love seemed to have used her. It did reach the boss's ears and Julie was duly reprimanded and warned. It also reached Nick's ears and Julie had to suffer the humiliation that her plan to prove something had backfired spectacularly. Needless to say she lost about ten pounds through worry and ended up looking ten years older than she was – too thin and drawn.

With time, effort and some recipes for emotional rescue, Julie managed to repair the damage from the break-up and her subsequent behaviour. In the end she learned to be gentler on herself, accepting that some bad behaviour was to be expected. And the message for you to take from this first case study is that on the whole people do recover from these episodes. It's OK – you're allowed a bit of crazy time after the break-up. You may drink too much (on occasion only), choose inappropriate partners, bore your best friends by droning on about your terrible ex and eat far too many cream cakes, or find it impossible to eat more than a tiny morsel as you're so wound up with emotion that you just can't stomach food!

What we want to stop is this negative behaviour becoming a bad break-up habit. We're going to turn you around and help you create some good break-up habits – these make up *The Break-Up Survival Kit*. If you haven't started any bad habits I may have caught you in the nick of time and you can channel all that break-up energy into doing something positive for yourself. What sort of things will be included in *The Break-Up Survival Kit?* Emotional rescue techniques like learning to seize the moment, making opportunities for yourself, developing curiosity about new people and getting rid of romantic biases and learning to face any social fears. And what is not in the kit? Destructive emotions directed inappropriately that end up damaging your self-esteem, and negative behaviour that compromises you as a person.

Let's take a moment to find out if you're guilty of making crazy or inappropriate decisions. Answer the following questions and then see where you stand – are you teetering on the brink of too much madness? Or are you reeling yourself in to safety?

The 3 D Quiz – how depressed, desperate or desolate are you acting?

Be *honest* in selecting the answer that best describes your behaviour. These questions are directed at the time *since* your break-up. Remember that it's no good selecting answers that sound rational if you haven't been behaving that way.

1) Have you binged on food *or* starved yourself in reaction to strong emotions?

   Yes or No

2) Have you made any regrettable phone calls/sent any inappropriate letters to your ex?

   Yes or No

3) Has your drinking increased or become unpredictable?

   Yes or No

4) Does your temper flare for no apparent reason?

   Yes or No

5) Have you had any sexual contact/experiences you regret?

   Yes or No

6) Do you find yourself falling in love too easily – with almost anyone who pays you attention?

   Yes or No

7) Have you 'come on' to somebody you shouldn't – like your boss?

   Yes or No

8) Do you fantasise about your ex dying in nasty circumstances/

going bald/getting some hideous affliction?
Yes or No

9) Have you ever felt scared witless for no apparent reason?
Yes or No

10) Has anyone (whose judgement you trust) told you that you're acting like a 'shrew', a 'bit mad' or 'bonkers', or out of control?
Yes or No

11) Have you destroyed any property, even though it was useful to you, knowing that it would upset your ex?
Yes or No

12) Are you guilty of 'cutting off your nose to spite your face' in terms of your ex in any way, shape or form?
Yes or No

1–3 'Yes' answers – You've reined in your worst impulses with only a few slip-ups along the way! Perhaps you've got a good 'crisis buddy' keeping an eye on you so that you don't destroy your self-respect. Or maybe you're winning the battle to do something positive after your break-up. Reading *The Break-Up Survival Kit* will help you continue along this path to making the most of your new life.

4–6 'Yes' answers – You're definitely behaving badly! Things may just get out of control. People may be worried about you at this point. And your ex may be laughing at the gossip they hear about you. You're a good candidate for *The Break-Up Survival Kit* – it can help get you back on to the straight and narrow.

More than 6 'Yes' answers – You're in danger of seriously damaging yourself, upsetting others and doing many things you may regret. You desperately need to take *The Break-Up Survival Kit* to heart. It's time to address some of your worst emotional impulses and destructive behaviour that are jeopardising your welfare. You can choose to heal your heart and mind and find a happier way of living with your break-up. Use any of the tips in the coming chapters to help improve your life.

Now it's time to get started with Chapter One. It's time to start seeing your ex for the person they were, not through a rose-coloured filter. In gaining this vision you will then see that they're not worthy of your emotional energy. You can now direct it into doing something positive for yourself.

FACING REALITY

Your ex was NOT the best thing since sliced bread, or worth wasting your energy on

In this first chapter we're going to begin with your ex! 'Why?' you may ask, 'should I focus on that good-for-nothing?' Or your immediate response may have been to feel a sudden knife-like feeling in your chest, a lump in your throat and tears in your eyes, as you think you can't cope with a whole chapter about 'that hurtful monster'. If these, or something similar, are your responses to thinking about your ex then you definitely need to confront these negative feelings that will hold you back from healing. You are the perfect candidate for *The Break-Up Survival Kit*! We don't want your heart and mind full of such pain simply when the topic of your ex comes up. You need to face the reality that, whether you'd take your ex back at the drop of a hat or you can't stand them, either way it's a waste of your precious emotional energy and it's time you were rescued.

Looking at your ex as a person

Now, how are we going to make this somewhat painful (or anger-arousing) task easier for you? The best way forward is to use a few techniques to help you focus on the fact that your ex was NOT the best thing since sliced bread – for those of you still pining for the days when you were together. Or, for those of you fuming at the thought of them, just how unworthy your ex is of your angry feelings.

It's important to note at this point that such inner feelings will permeate all of your 'being'. Without using *The Break-Up Survival Kit* these feelings could fester and start to influence your choices in daily life. Another thing to remember is that people gather a lot of clues about the inner workings of your mind *even* if you're not aware of it. As you start to meet new people, they are pretty good at sensing if you are someone who hasn't stopped longing for their ex, someone who's wasting their time in a romantic no-go zone where their heart and mind is filled with wistful longing for what once was – even if in reality that 'what' wasn't so great! Everything in your life is standing still, as if you're in the grip of some great waiting game. If truth be told most people are attracted to others who have things going on in their lives – not those who appear to be *existing* in abject misery. I say 'existing' because that's what your waiting, pining and longing trap you in – a miserable existence.

Too many people also get caught up in a cycle of loathing that prevents their hearts and minds from moving forward and opening up. *Potential* partners sense this anger and don't find it very pleasant. Friends and family also feel the brunt of the negativity because when you want to get back at an ex who has treated you badly but has long gone, who do you take these things out on? Your nearest and dearest! They're all quietly hoping you'll leave this hate behind while tiptoeing round you.

As a starting point, to get you thinking in the right direction, tick off the number of annoying, hurtful or spiteful things your ex was capable of.

The Ex-Factor Check List
Part One – Misbehaviour when we WERE together

- My ex never really listened to me
- My ex flirted with people in front of me
- My ex said nasty things to me
- My ex was cold in bed
- My ex was irresponsible with money
- My ex had bad breath/personal hygiene
- My ex treated his/her friends better than me
- My ex was unreliable (never rang when supposed to/late for meeting me, etc.)
- My ex had disgusting habits like nose-picking, nail-picking and snoring (give one tick for each of these you can name)
- My ex never did his/her share of household tasks
- My ex didn't treat our children well/think about them (allocate a double tick)
- My ex embarrassed me in front of people I cared about
- My ex could be emotionally or physically abusive (allocate a double tick)
- My ex drank too much/used illegal substances (allocate a double tick)
- My ex had an affair/s (allocate a double tick)

- My ex was boring
- My ex teased me about my shortcomings
- My ex called me upsetting names like 'Fatty!'
- My ex was scary when angry (allocate a double tick)
- My ex never cared about my sexual satisfaction
- Any other misbehaviour not listed above

Part Two – Misbehaviour DURING/AFTER the break-up

- My ex found someone new too quickly
- During the break-up my ex only thought of his/herself
- My ex took things that didn't belong to him/her
- My ex said nasty things about me
- My ex rubbed my nose in his/her happiness at leaving me
- My ex never returns calls/answers letters about sorting things out
- My ex tries to turn people against me
- My ex tries to upset me with phone calls, etc., at inappropriate times
- My ex is practically stalking me (he/she didn't want the break-up)
- My ex has infuriated me by taking up something I always wanted him/her to try
- I keep hearing from people how much my ex has changed – for the better!
- Add any other misbehaviour not listed above

Revising your view of your ex

Count up how many of these misbehaviours your ex was guilty of. Don't forget to include ones you've thought of but I've left off my list. I'd like you to underline all you've ticked in the book, write them out on a piece of paper and stick it somewhere you'll see it regularly. Perhaps one of the drawers left empty by your ex (and think of this as a positive – you have more space!).

3–5 ticks – Your ex wasn't the worst possible person but they've clocked enough ticks to be unworthy of your love. Remember that only one tick of a serious nature, e.g., 'was abusive' or 'had affairs', is enough to warrant you never entertaining any rose-coloured thoughts about them!

6–10 ticks – We're getting into more serious territory here. Your ex wasn't a very rewarding person to share your life with. In fact they were probably taking you for granted to the extent your relationship was doomed.

10+ ticks – You're very lucky to be out of there! You should be heaving a great sigh of relief that you aren't chained to this person. How could they be worth your emotional energy? If you're devoting your energy to them, read on for some advice of the emotional kind.

A good case of someone who was wasting emotional energy on an ex, who had far too many ticks on the Ex-Factor Check List is Fiona. I met Fiona when she'd been stuck mourning her unworthy ex for about four months. At 27 she seemed to be throwing away her chances of meeting someone new through her inability to move forward. The vibe she gave out was one of someone wrapped up in the past. It was obvious to any interested men that she simply wasn't emotionally available.

Why was she wasting her energy on her ex? He'd had a number of critical ticks on the Ex-Factor Check List including, being 'emotionally abusive', calling her 'nasty names' and caring 'more for his friends'. Adding these ticks together, it was understandable that Fiona's self-esteem had taken a terrible knock. Speaking honestly, she admitted that she was locked into trying to work out why the relationship had progressed in the way it had, fantasising about how things could have been different and wondering whether, if she was more assertive, she could make it work *even* now. Fiona also admitted that she was scared of it happening again. She didn't want to tempt fate by seeing anyone new and going through such unhappiness again. It really was a case of her longing for the devil she knew.

And what helped Fiona? It was helpful for her to put down in such clear terms all the 'ticks' her ex had against him. We also discussed challenging such negativity on her part. Fiona desperately needed a clear-out of the negative emotions in her heart and negative thoughts clouding her mind. *The Break-Up Survival Kit* would help Fiona do this and improve the vibe she gave out to potential partners.

How to renew the romance-vibe you GIVE out

Circle the words that apply to you. Does your vibe include:

ANGER   MISTRUST   DOUBTING ATTITUDE

SHYNESS   EMOTIONAL BARRIERS   SARCASM

CYNICISM   SNEERING   FEARFULNESS

NERVOUSNESS   TEARFULNESS

PLOTTING/SCHEMING   **VENGEFULNESS**

DEVIOUSNESS   **NEEDY**   **DEPENDENT**

LACK OF CONFIDENCE

Now let's do the visualisation technique that Fiona tried – close your eyes and imagine you were, for at least a moment, free enough *emotionally* to be on the look-out for potential dates. Imagine you spot somebody through your office window who you think is physically attractive. You hope they enter your place of work – and they do. Next, think what it would be like if you seized the moment and flirted with them because physically they were irresistible. But the moment they face you and start speaking, the body language, voice and facial expressions are full of cynicism, anger, shyness, mistrust, etc – all those words *you'd* circled above. Get the picture? Your initial optimism would be shattered immediately and if you were wise you'd give that person a wide berth. They're obviously not ready for dating!

Think about the romance-vibe you'd LIKE to give out

Look again at the words you've circled and now write out three new, positive words you're going to BE! For example, you may put down 'Happy', 'Open', and 'Confident'.

1/_____ 2/_____ 3/_____

It's important for you to recall this technique when you're out and about meeting people – give out the romance-vibe of the words of your choice! This is what you're going to work towards in three steps. One – recall your positive words! Two – take a couple of relaxing breaths to ground yourself! Three – remember you can *choose* to be someone who gives out a negative vibe or a positive one – it's in your power!

Next, Fiona needed to learn to separate her *reality*-based thoughts from her *fantasies* about her ex and what could be. Fantasies are funny things when it comes to emotional renewal. They can be very positive and can be put to good use to help you move forward. But they can hold you back when used as an escape mechanism (preventing you facing your new life) so that you dwell on 'could have beens', 'maybes' and 'what ifs'.

Identifying your negative fantasy life

People use fantasy negatively in many ways. The best way to identify the way fantasy is holding you back and filling you with negative, hope-destroying, false scenarios, is to keep a diary of your fantasy life for a few days. I've provided you with a page here:

First give it a fun title that'll make you smile. For example, 'My Outrageous Completely Unrealistic Fantasy Life'.

Your 'Ex-Fantasy' Diary Title: _____

My 'Ex-Fantasy'	When it occurred (I was bored, miserable, etc)	Could it really come true? (Yes? No? Be honest)
1)		
2)		
3)		

4)

5)

6)

Your new fantasy image _____

(Do NOT fill this in until you've taken the steps below)

Clearing out your ex-fantasies from your heart and mind

Take a look at your remarks across the three categories. In the first category, do your ex-fantasies revolve around the same theme? So are they always, e.g., 'My ex sweeps into my office and proclaims that he or she has made a huge mistake, validating me in front of my colleagues,' or, 'My ex dies of an excruciating heart attack in his or her favourite bar?' You know the sort of things I'm talking about. Or do they vary in content?

In the second category, do your ex-fantasies tend to occur when you're feeling a certain way? For example, something has not worked out so you use an ex-fantasy for escapism.

Finally, what are your honest, realistic opinions of the likelihood of your ex-fantasies coming true? Yes, I thought so! You know there's very little chance of these fantasies coming true. So it's time to put a check on them.

- Set a timer and allow yourself five minutes 'ex-fantasy time' per day. Sitting/lying quietly, focus completely on your most frequent ex-fantasy. Indulge your 'needy' self with these images.

- When time's up, clear your mind, sit up and have a good laugh at your self-indulgence! Scan your Ex-Factor Check List and believe all the negative ticks you've allocated your ex. Put your Ex-Fantasy Diary Sheet and Check List side by side and again look at the ticks and look at your fantasy – do they match up? No!

- Now, for the *you* that would like emotional rescue, it's time to create a new fantasy image. Imagine your perfect partner – someone who doesn't accumulate ticks on the Ex-Factor Check List! Someone who has the qualities that you'd expect in a loving partner. Enjoy this fantasy for a few moments. Once it's clear in your mind enter it on your diary sheet. When you catch yourself slipping into an ex-fantasy go through these steps and your diary sheet to re-boost your new, positive fantasy life that'll give you optimism.

Why are you stuck on your ex?

Whether you can't stand your ex (and dwell on them negatively) or you long to get your ex back, being stuck either way makes you a worthy candidate for *The Break-Up Survival Kit* in terms of cleansing your heart and mind. Why do so many people get stuck either in a haze of pitiful hope or trapped in their anger – crowding out all the positive emotional experience they could have in this new phase in their life? There are four main reasons why people get stuck at either end of this emotional spectrum:

1) Self-protection – It actually protects them in a funny sort of way! Yes, they get some sort of security from focusing their energy – sad or angry – on their ex. This way they never have to dip a toe in the romantic waters again, at least for the time being. It's so much easier to focus on someone who's out of your life than risk this pain again – by being prepared to take on someone new. Fiona, above, is a case in point.

Are you guilty of this?

1) Do you get anxious when you think about your future? Yes / No
2) Does it take you a while to warm to new people? Yes / No
3) If you **want** your ex back – do you fantasise that, if given the chance, you could make it work with your ex? **Or**, if you can't stand your ex, do you think burning off negative energy by directing it at them is helpful? Yes / No
4) Do you waste a lot of emotional energy worrying about things you can't change/control? Yes / No

'Yes' answers to three or four – You're likely to be a romantic self-protector!

Things to exclude from your heart and mind:

- Fearful feelings – throw them out! Identify them, e.g., 'I'll never find anyone else.' Then change them – 'I *will* find someone else!'
- Doubts about your date-ability! Honestly appraise your friends who date actively. Do they have some special quality that sets them apart? Probably not, except romantic optimism! They're people like you, but they simply believe they're worthy of some fun.
- Throw your caution to the wind. Force yourself to make the

first small move the next time you're attracted to someone. Try giving a simple smile or saying 'hello'.

Rescue strategies

- Build your confidence generally by setting small goals to aim for at work and socially.

- Do more of what you can do. Think back over your past. What nice things has anyone said about you? For example, have you been told you have a good sense of humour? Then work at it, hone it and practise some jokes and party pieces. Getting one positive thing under your belt will give you the courage to believe in your other positives.

- Create a self-affirmation that will help to guard you against scary, anxious thoughts. Try something like, 'Fear will get me nowhere, confidence will get me everywhere!' Write yours here:

_____

2) Creature of habit – Focusing on your ex quite simply becomes a bad break-up habit. We humans are creatures of habit and not all habits are good ones (think of cigarettes). So, sometimes we allow ourselves to be at the mercy of negative romantic behaviour. If allowed to continue long after the break-up it becomes so much a part of our character that unless we treat it as a habit that needs breaking, we get stuck! Think of all that wasted energy!

Are you guilty of this?

1) Do you tend to get stuck in a routine? Yes / No
2) Do friends have to drag you out? Yes / No
3) Are you the sort who's not really bothered/anxious about trying new things? Yes / No
4) If you **want** your ex back – Do you fantasise that life would be easier if you and your ex got back together? **Or**, if you can't stand your ex, do you think it's good to hold on to your angry feelings about your ex? Yes / No

'Yes' answers to three or four – You may be a creature of romantic habit!

Things to exclude from your heart and mind

* Your need for everything to be done 'by the book' has to be dumped! Learn to look at the options.
* Don't fear spontaneity. Instead, enjoy spontaneous moments.
* Start reminding yourself why your relationship didn't work.
* If you are angry with your ex – List the reasons. Tear this list up and toss it bravely in the trash letting your anger go with it.

Rescue Strategies

* Embrace the moment!
* Try something new each week, no matter how small.
* Surprise yourself by doing some 'people-watching' and try to spot potential dating material.

- Break a habit in another part of your life – like having to arrange your desk at work 'just so'.

3) **Attention-seeker** – Some people quite enjoy the fact that after the break-up they get loads of attention from friends and family. They risk losing that attention if they move on. Instead they see, almost at a subconscious level, that there is an emotional pay-off in being miserable. If you recognise yourself in this then it's time to realise that you're living only half a life. You'll never be fulfilled while revelling in the pity and concern of others. So you must acknowledge this neediness and use *The Break-Up Survival Kit* as much as everyone else – simply to rebuild your confidence in being valued for positive reasons.

Are you guilty of this?

1) If you **want** your ex back – do you fantasise about them begging you to come back? **Or**, if you can't stand your ex, do you dream of ways to show them up? Yes / No
2) Do you tend to suffer from envy? Yes / No
3) Will you do almost anything to get attention? Yes / No
4) Are you quick to judge others? Yes / No

'Yes' answers to three or four – You're likely to be a romantic attention-seeker!

Things to exclude from your heart and mind

- Stop trying to hog the limelight! Attention doesn't necessarily equal love.

- Banish the pitying support you get from others by telling them that things are changing.
- Rid yourself of fantasies/thoughts that your ex is revelling in the attention of new people/dates.
- Stop making snap judgements about potential partners/dating material.

Rescue strategies

- Give others the chance to shine. Their appreciation will boost the way you feel about yourself.
- Seek out things that make you feel good but don't involve you getting attention for them, e.g., hobbies that you enjoy privately.
- Affirm the fact that self-love must come from within and not be dependent on the approval of others. Your mantra should become, e.g., 'I shine from within!' Write your own here:_____

In moments of doubt focus on this mantra!

4) **Rose-coloured specs** – Finally, many people suffer from a rather large dose of 'rose-coloured spectacles', particularly when they're the one who has been dumped. Their self-esteem dips as they come to believe that actually their ex was some great 'catch' and perhaps they weren't worthy of such a 'catch'. With each new person they meet they filter out the possibilities and instead convince themselves that no-one can match that ex. The ex becomes imbued with an almost mystical power – an act no-one can follow! And, strangely enough, this rose-coloured behaviour can apply to dumpers too! Sometimes the dumper suddenly gets

cold feet and thinks the person they left behind was 'the one' and how could they have been so stupid as not to see it at the time!

Are you guilty of this?

1) Do you **always** try to see the best in others? Yes / No
2) If you want your ex back – do you fantasise about getting back together in very romantic circumstances? **Or**, if you can't stand your ex do you fantasise that they'll never be happy in love? Yes / No
3) Is romance the most important ingredient to you in a long-term relationship? Yes / No
4) Do you get fooled easily/taken advantage of by people? Yes / No

'Yes' answers to three or four – You're probably a romantic with rose-coloured spectacles!

Things to exclude from your heart and mind

- This may sound extreme but stop always trying to see the best in others! Sometimes you'll need to do a reality check to learn to accept that others aren't always thinking of *your* good.

- Stop bending the truth about the past – you're remaining stuck on your ex because you've allowed your 'perfect fantasy past' to take over your thoughts.

- Stop yourself from doom-making thoughts that no-one will ever be like your ex. Your ex was probably not your first

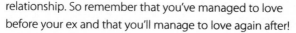

relationship. So remember that you've managed to love before your ex and that you'll manage to love again after!

- Don't defend your ex to others!

Rescue Strategies

- Emphasise what you have to offer rather than dwelling on what your ex had. Make a list of every positive attribute you have. Compare this to a list about your ex's negative qualities. (Yes, they *did* have them, you rose-coloured romantic!)
- Learn to rationalise fawning or over-romantic thoughts by debating these as they come into your mind. Have this debate with yourself, whether the thoughts are about your ex *or* someone you're interacting with in another part of your life.
- Immerse yourself in romantic novels, or simply watch other couples, and then play 'agony aunt' – where did the main characters go wrong in their pursuit of love? This will develop your skills of analysis.

Chapter conclusions: what the relationship-doctor ordered!

Hopefully you've begun to take on board the message of this chapter – namely that it's easy to get stuck being obsessive about, pining for, even hating your ex. None of these very different emotions will help you move on to enjoying your freedom. It's important that you recall the exercises to *exorcise* your ex from your heart and mind whenever you're feeling vulnerable or wobbly. Your heart and mind need an injection of positive energy, filling you with the belief that all is not lost, that you will enjoy love and romance again and that you as a person are worthy of a fulfilling relationship! Just to keep you on the straight and narrow fill in one *Break-Up Kit* affirmation for this chapter:

The most important thing I've learned about my ex and my feelings from this chapter is:

_____

_____

_____

And I'm going to remind myself of this!

SMOKE SIGNALS
The grand gestures we make to prove we're moving on

It's time to turn our attention to how others have handled their reactions to the breakdown of a relationship. We can learn so much about the break-up process from others' reactions. After a time, which is different for everyone, people usually want to signal to the world that they're moving on. These symbolic gestures say to the world, their ex, and themselves, 'I can make it! I'll survive! Look at the new me!' If we take a closer look at such gestures they very often reflect the core reason for the break-up. Generally, people tend to go to extremes with these gestures in an attempt to prove they're more than AOK with the break-up.

I like to call these gestures smoke signals because they are there to mask, hide and cover the pain the person is still obviously suffering but doesn't want to admit to, as well as sending out a message. You might assume these smoke signals are carefully orchestrated for maximum effect. However, sometimes they originate at a subconscious level – the person is actually still in so much pain that they don't realise the obvious message they're giving out. As an example let's take a fairly common occurrence in the world of heartbreak. Let's say your best friend's husband dumps her for another woman, who just happens to have a short, flirty haircut. A few days later your friend shows up with her lovely locks shorn and a new dramatic look. Perhaps too dramatic, like Brigitte Nielsen's (Sylvester Stallone's ex) near skinhead look. It's obvious to everyone *but* your friend that the style she's chosen reflects one of the, at least outward, reasons for the break-up – that she can look like the person her ex actually wanted. It's become a sort of subconscious 'so there!' gesture.

Others who send smoke signals have a target in mind for the message they're sending. For example, when Vanessa Feltz was so publicly dumped by her husband, she immediately set to work transforming herself into the new chic and sleek woman she has become. Vanessa appeared to know exactly what she was doing. She wanted to tell the world, and even more so her ex, that she was now a 'babe who won't be two-timed again!'

It's fascinating to see such celebrity changes documented in the press – it gives us mere mortals in the death throes of a relationship some sort of role model – 'If they can survive and change in a positive way, so can I!' Seeing Vanessa Feltz literally shrinking before your eyes week by week is fascinating and inspiring. It gives you hope when you're newly single and looking for emotional rescue – even if your way through the break-up doesn't involve food and weight loss.

Liz Taylor, on the level of the international celebrity, has provided us with a physical barometer of the successes and failures of her marriages over the years. Who needs celebrity gossip when you can simply look at a snap of her at some showbiz 'do' and guess that if she's slim it must be 'love time', if she's heavy it must be 'dump time'. Liz has appeared to take the opposite course to Vanessa when it comes to romantic smoke signals. Her weight seemed to betray her need for comfort food after a break-up and it has been said that her spending reaches dizzy heights at this point, too. Apparently Liz will purchase fabulous jewels during a break-up as if to send a smoke signal saying 'I don't need *his* money to buy me presents – I can choose my own!' when perhaps what she's really thinking is 'I feel so hurt but I'm not going to show him!'

Spending money inappropriately is a smoke signal that can go terribly wrong. Of course the finances of Sarah Ferguson, the Duchess of York, have been well documented. It appears that her spending shot up as her marriage to Prince Andrew collapsed. Such spending seemed to cocoon her from the unhappiness she was experiencing in the aftermath of the break-up. However, in the end it proved an even bigger nightmare for her. That's why it's best to consider the nature and repercussions of any smoke signals you choose to send. They'll only be part of a good *Break-Up Survival Kit* if you learn something about yourself, or if they move you on to finding really constructive action to take.

A unique smoke signal was given out by Liz Hurley when she and Hugh Grant finally decided to take an official break from each other in June 2000. Liz was photographed with a large tropical snake draped seductively around her scantily clad body. The message this sent, loud and clear, was 'After Hugh, I'm looking for something a little more dangerous!' Celebrities often use such break-up opportunities to launch a new look or as publicity for a new project. In Liz's case it simply seemed to be an advertisement for being back on the singles market. It appeared that her emotional rescue was going to come in the shape of a new type of man.

At the time of writing Liz and Hugh have been seen looking quite cosy again unless of course Liz has been hiding some dangerous, different type of guy in the background. Sometimes the smoke signals we send may not have the expected pay-off. They may even communicate a message to an ex that they find irresistible and you end up back together – we'll have to wait and watch with Liz and Hugh!

But how about the rest of us who aren't in the public eye? We don't have the general public interested in our smoke signals but we still inhabit our own very important world and wish to signal those involved in our lives. I'd like to tell you about Gillian. She was an attractive 37-year-old who'd had a messy divorce from her husband of 12 years. No third party was involved in the actual divorce, which was quite simply due to them having drifted apart to the point that they were strangers sharing a home. James also had become rather engrossed in his work as the marriage deteriorated.

After their separation Gillian started hearing how her ex, James, was being seen around with a number of attractive women. Inside Gillian was seething. She felt that he'd paid so little attention to her in the last couple of years of their marriage but now he had all the time in the world for women. What was Gillian's smoke signal? She started dressing like a . . . well, I've got to be frank . . . like a complete tart. Her once rather quiet, but attractive style went out the window. She immediately substituted eye-catching numbers in loud colours and not much material and with perhaps too many shiny, dangly things attached. It really was disco diva stuff. I think you can get the picture.

After a couple of months of prancing around in the highest of shoes, shortest of skirts and too much make-up, Gillian came down to earth. Her smoke signal days were over and although she zapped up her old image a little she dumped the extremes of her new look. Really there was no harm done. Gillian had got over the worst of her need to show the world she could be 'exciting' and could now concentrate on the real *Break-Up Survival Kit*. That was to take stock of her life. Enjoy its good points and build in more of these and leave behind the blander aspects – like the book club

James had persuaded her to join a couple of years earlier, but which she really found dull. I might add it had been rather convenient for him getting Gillian involved in things while he threw himself into his work!

It's important to note that men give out smoke signals too. A good case in point, mirroring Gillian's, is Jonathon. Jonathon was one of these really 'nice' guys who doesn't always get the girl because he was so nice. Unfortunately he'd played the 'doormat' in a couple of relationships but with Joanne he thoughts things were different. They hadn't married but had lived in relative happiness for 18 months when she dropped the bombshell that she was moving on. Jonathon may have been nice but he wasn't stupid. He pieced together the fact that Joanne had cared for him but that really he'd been a break from the more exciting type of men she actually preferred.

Jonathon's deeper sense of 'who he was' felt challenged. Was he destined to always be the 'nice guy' that most women wanted as a friend but not a lover? No, he was going to take action – and hoped to send smoke signals out about the new Jonathon. He decided to venture to the local men's boutique to find a look that would make him appear more exciting. It was no more Mr Nice Guy as he ended up looking like a pimp. Not a very comfortable one at that as he squirmed in his tight leather trousers and silky shirt.

Jonathon found, even more quickly than Gillian, that he was not comfortable with the smoke signals he was sending. He finally found a middle ground as he turned to a Break-Up Survival Kit to build his confidence. Jonathon could be nice without being a pushover. This new-found confidence actually was rather attractive to the women he started to meet. A lesson for us all, that confidence in yourself can be a magnet for the right sort of attention.

How high is your confidence right now?

Take this quick quiz and be completely honest!

1) How important is the approval of others to you?
   A) It's quite important – I feel much better if I have it
   B) It's very important. I feel upset without approval.
   C) It's important only in certain circumstances.

2) If a friend wanted to set you up on a blind date how would you react?
   A) I'd go for it but feel wary.
   B) I'd feel flustered and nervous. They'd probably have to twist my arm.
   C) I'd definitely go for it even if I felt nervous.

3) How much do you dwell on your appearance?
   A) I probably think about my appearance too much.
   B) I constantly worry/am obsessed about my appearance.
   C) I get myself ready and get on with my day.

4) Do you think your ex is having a better time than you?
   A) My ex might be having a better time.
   B) I'm sure my ex is having a better time.
   C) I don't think my ex is having a better or a worse time than me.

5) When you have to make a decision what happens?
   A) It takes time for me to make one.
   B) I go over and over my options, feeling unsure of any, and worry about my choices.
   C) I can make decisions quite easily.

Mainly As – Cautiously confident! Things could be better but you seem to be aware of that. That's the first step to renewing your confidence. Now take a look at the advice above to keep you on track.

Mainly Bs – Collapsing confidence! Your confidence has taken a severe knock and you need to renew it.

* Think of your top two qualities and any time you're feeling wobbly remind yourself of these.

* If self-doubting thoughts cross your mind replace them with 'I've survived so far – I can make it!'

* Take one day at a time. Thinking ahead to an entire future 'on your own' is a negative fantasy and something you can't predict.

* Set yourself a small goal each day so you feel that you're getting on with things. One day it may relate to work, another day to your friends. Write them down as you accomplish them. You'll be surprised how fast the list grows.

* Recall the last thing you did well. Was it something your boss praised you for? Did a friend appreciate some advice/help? When you are feeling useless remember that you aren't!

* When faced with decisions write out your top two options. Go through the pros/cons of each, then make your choice. Think through what could be the worst possible outcome if your choice fails – you'll probably find it's something you can cope with!

Mainly Cs – Calm and confident! No matter what stage in the break-up you're at, your confidence is intact at present. Keep making decisions, be aware of anxieties and face them as they arise. Affirm yourself and keep stopping any fantasy thoughts that your ex is having a grand time.

The cycle of change

Smoke signals are an important part of the cycle of learning to accept that things need to change. Part of confidence-boosting after the break-up is that you can survive change. What happens is that often people end up taking a few steps too far with the signals they send and feel overwhelmed. They're going in the right direction but at a breathless pace without stopping to think because they are being driven purely at an emotional level. Smoke signals symbolise a period of adjustment, or even a fighting spirit so in that sense they are definitely positive – unless of course you end up looking like a tart or pimp, broke or not nourishing yourself properly. But it is better to take action than to sink into the feeling that life is too awful or too hard to change.

Another good case for the guys is Sam. His ex-wife had accused him of being a complete bore. She was quite sporty and frankly Sam was a bit of a couch potato. Their break-up was acrimonious and Sam was left feeling that no other woman would want him. Rather than turning to a positive *Break-Up Survival Kit* and getting into shape in a measured way, Sam decided to become Action Man! He took up shotokan karate – a highly physical martial art – even though he hadn't seen the inside of a gym for years. But what better smoke signal than to say, 'Look at me – when the going gets tough, I'll get tough!' Needless to say with that gung-ho attitude, but out of shape body, Sam had a broken hand in the first week of karate training! The moral to this tale is that sometimes we suffer for our smoke signals in unexpected ways.

How to see through others' smoke signals

 They mention their ex with every 'new-me' statement. For example, they say things like 'My ex didn't appreciate the "party me"!' as they whirl around the dance floor with their sixth partner of the evening.

- People whisper about how much they've changed in such a short time.
- You have a sense that you're talking to someone who's hiding their real self. Listen to your intuition!
- They change abruptly in one way or another after a drink or two. They slip back into their 'real self'.
- You visit their home and their 'look' is not reflected in their domestic set-up.
- They have a nervous laugh, twitch, or perspiration that belies the fact they're playing a part – sending out smoke signals.
- You've heard, or know, that they're trying their hardest to let their ex know about the changes in their life.
- They frequently ask for others' approval of their new 'look' or attitude.

How to recognise when you're going over the top with your own smoke signals

- More than one friend/family member questions your new style.
- You notice eyebrows rise as you walk in with your new look.
- You can't quite believe what you're wearing, doing, eating or withholding from yourself.
- You've become obsessed in your inner thoughts about your ex hearing of the 'new you'.
- Someone you haven't seen recently barely recognises you.
- Your food bill has markedly increased (due to comfort eating as if to say 'I don't care what anyone thinks, I'll eat what I want!') or decreased (you're trying to prove a point by

shrinking your clothing size). Or your clothing size has changed (either direction) by more than one size without you thinking of the nutritional implications.

- You sense people are talking about you, perhaps at work, and perhaps too much.
- Other aspects of your life are taking second place to the new aspect – your smoke signal's taking over!

Rescue strategies for smoke-signal restraint

! Repeat the following statement, shaping it to suit your smoke signal: 'I'll think carefully before I keep taking action in this direction!'

! If you went in for wardrobe changes, tone down your choice the next time you're out by one fashion 'step'. That is, if you've gone for the 'tart' or 'pimp' look retain the short skirt but leave out the slashed-to-the-waist top (for the former). Retain the powerful aftershave but lose the leather trousers (for the latter).

Tips for going for that new attitude

! Try some wigs on before going for that bold new haircut to ensure that it suits you.

! Check if you can bend over in your new shorter skirts without breaking the decency laws.

! Guys – check out your new, tight, black leather, Ricky Martin-style trousers won't raise your voice an octave!

I Remember that Brad Pitt can get away with the stubbly unshaven look but do a reality check – do you have his face shape or the star quality to get away with it?

I Sticking with the image of Brad Pitt, he can get away with the rough look in his movies and wear tattoos all over the shop. But can you, in your life? Were you tempted by the rough look when your ex called you a wimp? Even if you want to portray a 'manly, no-one's-going-to-break-this-heart-again look' it doesn't mean you'll succeed with such extremes!

I If you went in for spending for comfort, e.g., to achieve a new look or take a holiday, take a look at your credit cards and bank balance. Get in touch with your bank's financial advisor to get your spending back on track. If your smoke signals are impulsive cut up your credit cards before you get into any more trouble. Look at creating new looks by combining clothes you already have in different ways so that you don't feel you have to purchase more.

I Hold back on that last drink when you've decided that alcohol makes you more 'exciting'. I've got news for you – it probably doesn't!

I If your smoke signal involves weight loss or gain pay particular attention to Chapter Six – The Divorce Diet.

I Think of ways to achieve *emotional* rescue through smoke signals rather than dwelling on physical changes. These may involve taking up a hobby or interest you always wanted to. Think of the fun you could have learning something new. It's great for your self-esteem and is a smoke signal of sorts. Your ex may hear that you're doing something fun, different, or exciting – and how much you're enjoying it. But who cares what they think anyway? Let's move on to Chapter Three where we'll delve into permanent changes after the break-up – and how these can help you.

The most important thing I've learned from this chapter about the smoke signals I might be sending is: _____
_____
_____

And I'm going to remind myself of this!

3

THE CHAMELEON FACTOR
What you should and shouldn't change

In Chapter One we looked at your ex's behaviour and some of the reasons why you might be reacting to it. In Chapter Two we looked at some famous and not-so-famous smoke signals to relationship breakdown. So now it's time to take a closer look at you and how you're reacting to the break-up of your relationship. As I like to encourage people to learn to adapt and change as new circumstances arise after a break-up, I call this the Chameleon Factor. Think of the chameleon – an amazing creature able to change and adapt to its environment for its own purposes and benefit. The chameleon gets on with its life in the best possible way and that's what you need to do.

I find it quite helpful to begin by breaking this into three parts – what you are thinking, what you are feeling and what you are doing. Then we'll look at what you *should* be thinking, feeling and doing in order to survive your break-up and how these might apply to really changing your life. This chapter will also be about fine-tuning your behaviour after the break-up. In the last chapter we showed how OTT behaviour can be incredibly symbolic and sometimes helpful – to a point! But we can't continually go around waving these huge flags of 'victory' – our smoke signals. At some point, things have to calm down; we have to tone down the smoke signals and make change workable for our individual lifestyles.

Let's begin by breaking down what's actually going on with you in your post-break-up life. Then we can look at handling change and make decisions that will enhance your life.

What you are *thinking*

Hands up if you've **thought/are thinking** any of the following:

- I'll never find love again
- My ex was the worst thing that could ever have happened to me
- I'll never recover from the damage of the break-up
- I think I've had enough of trying
- I'll never trust again

. ... thinking these sorts of thoughts – Yes / No (please circle)

What you are *feeling*

Hands up if you've **felt/are feeling** any of the following:

- I'm hateful, I loathe myself
- I feel useless, stupid, idiotic
- I feel desperate, lonely, devastated
- I feel no-one will ever love me
- I feel hopeless

. ... feeling these sorts of things – Yes / No (please circle)

What you are *doing*

Hands up if you've **done/are doing** any of the following:

- I'm eating too much/not enough
- I'm not looking after myself
- I'm chewing my nails, picking my cuticles, pulling my hair
- I'm drinking too much, taking legal drugs inappropriately, and/or using illegal drugs
- I'm not sleeping well/sleeping too much
- I'm acting obsessively in any way
- I'm not doing my job properly, or carrying out my responsibilities well enough
- I'm not being a good enough parent

I'm doing these sorts of things – Yes / No (please circle)

How many Yes answers did you circle? Three, two or *even* one circle may mean that trouble is brewing for your rescue. These thoughts, feelings, actions and behaviours all indicate that you need to start chucking the rubbish – the emotional junk food – out of your heart and mind. And instead you should embark on a course of emotional rescue that will become a constant in your way of conducting your life. You may believe at some sort of *wishful* level, 'What I'm doing is really not so bad.' This means you need to do a reality check!

Doing a reality check

I believe that doing reality checks is important. Your attitudes need to be right to cope with changes to come. But you may wonder how to go about doing this at a practical level. Try this: imagine a friend, family member, or even a work colleague who's recently gone through a break-up. Now what if *they* were thinking, feeling or doing the things you have ticked. Perhaps they've suddenly lost weight or started sleeping around or drinking too much. They're also running themselves down with negative thoughts and feelings. You'd think that they needed to take positive action to begin a recipe of emotional renewal.

NOW holding these thoughts in your mind – please tick one of the following:

I deserve the same emotional rescue as this friend/family member

I DON'T deserve the same emotional rescue as this friend/ family member

Now, if you HAVEN'T ticked the first option I'll be very surprised! At the rational level I'm sure you absolutely believe you deserve the same rescue after your break-up as the next person. But, if part of you, for some negative reason, believes that you still have to keep hurting, I'd like to know why you are any different. And why you are allowing yourself to ignore the fact that you could be moving towards a better, happier place.

Fill this in:

Why I am different _____

I hope that is still blank – that you could NOT come up with a good reason for not allowing yourself the chance to start down the road of emotional rescue.

Perhaps at a deeper level of consciousness you've got this uncomfortable feeling, possibly your intuition, that is trying to tell you something. You may feel that your 'new look' could get you quite a lot of trade on a street corner. Or that that new larger-than-life, party-animal attitude is going to attract the wrong kind of attention (and gossip!). But part of you still feels inclined to go for it. This means that an essential part of you is still stuck at the smoke signal stage. It indicates that your emotional need to show the world, your ex and yourself that you 'mean business' is still dominating the flow of your life rather than allowing yourself the chance to take more considered action that may lead to more satisfying change and results. It wouldn't hurt for you to refresh yourself with the advice given in the last chapter on pages 33–38.

What you should change

As you embark on the Chameleon Factor – changing things to suit the demands of your new life – there are some ingredients to include in your emotional rescue. Let's begin with fine-tuning your attitudes to change and leave the biggest issues until later.

Your motto for change

The first step in adopting the most positive attitude to changing your thoughts, feelings and actions is to adopt your own 'motto for change'. This will reaffirm every day what you're trying to do. During my break-up, I adopted the motto 'I can face change without fear.' Every time I felt a pang of fear that I couldn't cope with something that my ex had done in our relationship or during the break-up, I repeated this and thought carefully about the action I could take.

Now take a moment to invent your own motto and write it here:

My motto for change:_____

Think of your motto any time you feel fearful or doubt yourself. You know the sorts of things I mean – lying awake in the dead of night thinking you'll never kick-start your life or that you're the only person in the world feeling this huge emotional pit of despair and desolation – and that it'll never change.

Make changes and take action!

Think about what change means to you in relation to your break-up. I'm sure you'll agree with me that change equals action. This can take so many forms: you could be faced with a really big life change like having to move home, which means taking lots of action. Let's list a few of these actions: finding a new place to live, packing up the old place, dividing your possessions, finding new schools (if you have children), investigating where shops are located, registering with a new doctor, etc. Other actions would include informing everyone of your move, getting a new phone number, sorting out gas and electricity, etc. Having to make such changes and take such action is very scary, particularly if your self-esteem has taken a blow.

But change and action can also be frightening when dealing with the smaller things in life. Keeping a set of spare fuses, tending the window boxes and getting out from the attic the Christmas decorations and putting them up may have all been done by your ex. When added to your own vast list, taking on board such activities seems like a huge amount of change in your routine and subsequent action to take.

Leslie came to see me in an anxious state about how she would cope with all the things her ex used to do. They had two children and had both worked. Life had always been full. But now that her ex only had the children every other weekend Leslie was beginning to get panic attacks about all the change she was experiencing and action this necessitated. Prior to the break-up Leslie had been unhappy but she'd never experienced such self-doubt. Now, she was lying awake in the middle of the night fretting about how she'd cope (and in doing this wasting her valuable energy!). Leslie needed to adapt and change.

Five-point adapting action strategy

Leslie and I worked out a five-point Adapting Action Strategy that entailed the following:

! Leslie kept a note of the changes she had to make that she *worried* about. These ranged from worrying about getting the school uniforms ironed, to how she'd get the children to their different Saturday morning activities – she couldn't be in two places at once and they weren't old enough to travel on their own.

! The notes Leslie kept allowed her to see a pattern emerge and then to prioritise the actions necessary to cope with her changing life. She decided to prioritise anything that directly related to the children's happiness. Their Saturday gym and ballet *did* matter to their happiness; having perfectly ironed clothes *didn't*!

! Leslie's motto for change became 'Change for the children is my priority.' When she fretted about something less important she reminded herself of this.

! As Leslie had particular problems relaxing at night, she needed to allow herself to let go then. She kept a notepad at her bedside where she sat quietly and wrote out any additional action she needed to take the next day and the next day only. You don't need to think a week ahead at bedtime. Once they were written down, she was to talk herself into letting go. Her action list was ready and now she *deserved* some peace of mind.

• If her thoughts still wandered anxiously she was to visualise her hand rising as if to say 'STOP!' Then she substituted what had come into her mind with a relaxing image – she selected an outing she'd had with her children. Leslie visualised them all laughing together. She held this image until she began to relax into sleep.

As time passed, Leslie found it easier to confront what panicked her and managed to get the panic attacks under control. Seeing in practice how she could cope with change and take action herself was a tremendous confidence booster. And it can be for you too.

An example of adapting action for you

I'd like you to think about the day-to-day sort of change you have to go through that plays on your mind. Write it down here, e.g., 'I am afraid of not getting my work finished from day to day as there are so many things to do, due to the break-up.'_____

_____

_____

Now work through the five-point adapting action strategy. If you're still anxious after prioritising the day-to-day change you're facing, think about this:

What is the worst thing that can happen if you don't quite get through everything? You're *not* going to fall off the edge of the earth, are you? Life won't crumble if your children don't get to all their lessons, or something at work gets left to the last minute.

And what's the best thing that can happen? Don't forget that in your new life, where you're adapting to change and taking action, the most important thing is sharing a laugh/cuddle with your children (if you have any), or friends, or family, and giving yourself a big emotional 'hug' for fighting your fear and moving on after the break-up.

Break-up survival technique for handling the bigger picture

Your first step to coping with the bigger issues of change is to define your Essential Life Areas. Essential Life Areas (ELAs) are the main strands of your life. Everyone has a slightly different combination. After my divorce, mine were my children, my work, my family, my friends and leisure – in that order. You may not have children, so that wouldn't be an ELA for you. You may combine friends and leisure together. I don't, as my friendships tend to be of a very emotionally connected type and my leisure area concerns sports and other activities of a more solitary type.

Your Essential Life Areas pyramid:

I'd like you to fill in this pyramid, placing your most important ELA at the top and working downwards to your least important. In my ELA pyramid my children were at the top. Even if you have children you may not put them at the top because, for example, they may be doing quite well (maybe you have your mum around the corner who provides a constant in their life) and it's your work that is falling apart or you need to train for something as you've been out of the work force for years.

1._____

2._____ 3. _____

4._____ 5. _____ 6._____

Once you've filled in the ELA pyramid you need to focus on how you spend your emotional energy in terms of these areas and how you should break down the time you give to each. It's helpful for your Break-Up Survival to make a note of the time you have available during an average week. Perhaps it's one hour per evening after you've taken care of all your responsibilities. Then decide how best these hours are used in the ELA areas, giving priority to number 1 and working downwards. This exercise may focus your mind and stop you from frittering away valuable time.

Time I may use during the week towards my emotional rescue:

Monday _____ hr/min
ELA to devote this to _____

Tuesday_____ hr/min
ELA to devote this to _____

Wednesday _____ hr/min
ELA to devote this to _____

Thursday _____ hr/min
ELA to devote this to _____

Friday _____ hr/min
ELA to devote this to _____

Saturday _____ hr/min

ELA to devote this to _____

Sunday _____ hr/min

ELA to devote this to _____

Now what issues form the bigger picture in terms of change in your life? Although I advise people not to rush into any big changes, I do think that, when all the cards have been thrown into the air with a major break-up, before they land around your feet and set into a fixed pattern, you may wish to consider whether this is a good time to make other changes. You may already know where some major changes are going to take place. For example, you're going to have to move from the 'relationship home' to live somewhere else. However, other things may not be so obvious. So, what are the sorts of areas I'm thinking of? They are your children (if any), career and/or training, friendships, new relationships, travel, new goals, attitudes and outlook, and any other major life area that applies to you.

You will already have an idea of how these fit in your present life, having thought through them in relation to your ELA pyramid. But now it's time to think how change is possible to reflect your new lifestyle.

How to rate your feelings about these areas

Rate each area on these three major dimensions: satisfaction, stimulation and how far they stretch you. For example, your career may stimulate you but not actually *stretch* you. The rating should be 1 to 5 where 1 = lowest score and 5 = highest score.

	Satisfaction	*Stimulation*	*Stretch Me*
Children:			
Career:			
Travel:			
Moving:			
Friendships:			
New relationships:			
New goals:			
Attitudes/outlook:			

Please note that for some areas, e.g., 'children' and 'stimulation', you need to think creatively. It can work either way – are you stimulating them enough or are you stimulated enough yourself as a parent? Similarly with 'children' and 'stretch me' – are you stretching to be the best possible parent you can be or are you stretching them enough? The point being that your own interpretation and rating is the most important.

Next, you need to examine the table and consider the following three Change Elements for any area that is rated 2 or 1 (low scores).

Rescue strategy – Change Element 1

Does this rating reflect directly on the break-up? For example, you may have rated career satisfaction as a '1' because you've been so emotionally drained that everything has got on top of you at work – and so you're not satisfied! Or does this relate to some career dissatisfaction that existed prior to the break-up or has developed at the same time but is not related to the break-up?

CE 1 – Fill in both parts:
Ratings of 2 or 1 that relate to the break-up (eg. children):____
Ratings of 2 or 1 that DON'T relate to the break-up:_____

Rescue strategy – Change Element 2

The next CE to consider is what you already have at your fingertips to start changing any areas rated 2 or 1. Looking at each individual area, you need to think in both practical terms (e.g. 'At my place of work they offer extra training for those keen to move up the ladder' – so you could arrange to take advantage of this) and emotional terms (e.g. 'If I could learn to stop being afraid of meeting new people I'd find it easier to start dating again' – so you could put in practice your own five-point adapting action plan to face this fear and change).

CE 2 – Fill in both parts:
Ratings of 2 or 1 where I can take practical steps:_____
Ratings of 2 or 1 where I can take emotional steps:_____

Rescue strategy – Change Element 3

Are there ratings of 2 or 1 where you don't have the necessary practical or emotional 'know-how' at your fingertips to improve these? If so, are you going to have to be creative in your solutions? Or perhaps you'll have to map out step-by-step goals to accomplish what you'd like to change. List the areas where you are going to take positive action that will require you to think creatively or plan the necessary steps to take.

CE 3 – Fill in both parts:
Ratings of 2 or 1 where I'll have to think creatively:

_____

One creative idea to start with: (brainstorm here!):

_____

Ratings of 2 or 1 where I can work out a step-by-step plan:

Step 1:_____

Step 2:_____

Step 3:_____

Now let's do a quick check to see if you are developing the Chameleon Factor – whether your attitudes to change are growing more positive.

Quiz: Are you ready for constructive change?

True or False – answer honestly!

1) I'm getting more *excited* and *less* scared about changes in my life. True / False
2) The most recent time my plans had to change abruptly I coped well. True / False
3) Life changes are more likely to make you a stronger person. True / False
4) Sometimes even the closest friendships/relationships undergo change. True / False
5) I can get anxious/nervous feelings under control when faced with something new. True / False

If you selected all the True answers you are well on your way to accepting change and taking action. A few things to remember if you chose some False answers:

!   You will conquer your fears about change if you follow the advice in this chapter.

- Seize the moment the next time a new opportunity arises – no matter how small. For example, if someone new at work asks you to join them for coffee, do it – don't be shy.

- Never be a slave to the routine of your life. Routine does give us some comfort and also helps our children survive the break-up. But it should never be so rigid as to make you scared of a little change or taking action.

- One by one, look at things you are thinking, feeling or doing that are stopping you from healing your pain (recheck the lists above). Tackle them in an order you feel comfortable with.

- Build in one new activity a week that applies to your ELA pyramid or the bigger picture of your life. It may be part of a number of steps to doing something new with, for example, your career.

- Never punish yourself for trying something new that doesn't work, or failing to effect some sort of change. The fact that you tried deserves tons of praise!

- Have fun! Yes – YOU! Build a little fun into your busy life and you'll feel more positive when faced with the need to change and take action.

- Recall the smoke signal days – it may have been a heady experience pretending to be someone you're not, but how long can you keep up a false exterior? For example, if you're normally shy, how long could you continue to bound into parties dressed to 'thrill', chat up every single person there and run home feeling drained from the experience? It is much better to fine-tune your own unique style, e.g., learn to flirt a little (something we'll discuss in the next chapter!), and build your long-term confidence, than to fling all your energies away on the short-term burn-out!

The most important thing I've learned from this chapter about adapting to change after my break-up is:

_____

_____

And I'm going to remind myself of this!

4

SEX AND THE NEWLY SINGLE

After the break-up of an important relationship, people often think that sex will be the last thing on their minds. The idea of being single again seems daunting – but sex as a single? Ooh, that's really frightening! However, once you're on the road to emotional rescue, the sexual side of new relationships becomes a possibility – at least in theory. Although you may think that emotional rescue is the most important part of your new life, your sexual self shouldn't be left to wither, cowering under scary, insecure feelings about your desirability. Instead, this chapter is all about helping you to rediscover your sexual self. Pleasing yourself and facing new sexual relationships are challenging for someone whose heart has been broken. But you can begin this important journey here and now.

Why is sex important?

Our experience as human beings covers a rich tapestry of events – all interwoven in an ever-shifting pattern that reflects our lives. Which of these events we emphasise in our lives determines the way we define ourselves. If you've emphasised the importance of your relationships in defining yourself (and, presumably, since you're reading *The Break-Up Survival Kit* this indicates that relationships are important to you) then undoubtedly part of this definition includes your sexual self.

In the long run, the happiest people are those who nurture all the important aspects of their lives. Therefore, even if you relegate sex to a low position on your list of priorities in the aftermath of a break-up, at some point real intimacy with another person may become more relevant. Also, if it's your sexual confidence that is low at this point, rebuilding is important because it may impact on the rest of your confidence.

Why does our sexual confidence take such knocks?

Our sexual confidence can take a knock after a break-up for a number of reasons. Depending on the reason for a break-up, people may find that their sexual interest, desire or even function diminishes. Imagine if your ex had an affair with someone who was younger and, as you imagine, sexier too. Your sexual confidence would take a nosedive like the best of kamikaze pilots! You may feel that simply by this choice of new partner your ex is making a statement to you – sending you a smoke signal sneering, 'Look what I've got, baby!'

It may be a more subtle reason that leads to diminished sexual confidence. Perhaps you and your ex simply drifted apart before the break-up. Sex became very boring and routine until it dwindled to nothing. There was no emotional connection and this led to diminished desire. Such circumstances may leave you with a blasé or fearful attitude towards getting intimate with someone. Inside your heart of hearts you start to ask, 'Will sex ever be good again?'

Another possibility is that, even if you and your ex had a good sex life, the general malaise and stress caused by a break-up can suddenly dent your interest in sex.

Often when sexual confidence takes a knock people start to make inappropriate choices. For example, you may feel that if you don't grab sex when it's on offer then you'll never have it again. Or you may fear being rejected by a new partner if you keep them waiting while you decide whether or not you're 'up to' the sexual side of a relationship. No-one should ever choose to have sex for such reasons! It should always be from a position of confidence and a sense of control.

The two stages of sexual rescue

Rescuing your sexual self really takes place in two stages. First, you need to be ready to flirt and have fun again and date a potential partner. And, secondly, you need to be ready for sex itself. Let's begin by looking at whether or not you're ready to date again.

How to tell if you're ready to date

Select the answer that best describes you and your behaviour at present:

1) Does most of your conversation with friends/family revolve around your ex? Yes / No
2) Do you feel sheer fear at the thought of opening up to someone new? Yes / No
3) I *don't* look at people I meet as potential dating material. Agree / Disagree

4) I feel uncomfortable/anxious when someone flirts with me.
Yes / No

5) I've said 'No' too quickly when someone asked me for a date recently. Yes / No

Three or more Nos/Disagrees and you're getting ready to date again! Otherwise, you may still be too troubled by the break-up to do justice to dating.

Rescue strategies to renew your 'date-ability'.

☼ Only allow yourself 10 minutes 'ex' time per day. Focus only on your ex. Imagine their face, their voice and mannerisms. Give yourself over completely to these thoughts. When your ten minutes is up, resolve to cut them out of your mind. Next week shorten this to five minutes. This will help if your ex is still too much a part of your emotional life – not a good start for dating!

☼ Like a film running through your mind, visualise yourself on a really successful date. Maybe it can be modelled on a date from the past where you were on sparkling form, or just simply based on how you'd like to appear to a date. Play this through your mind and see how date-able you really are. You *can* be like that when you finally date.

☼ Your dating aura – construct an affirmation about yourself as a potential date. It has to highlight all your romantic positives. For example, when I started dating again I thought, 'I have a great sense of humour and zest for life!' I held this thought in my mind whenever I felt doubtful about dating again. Construct yours here:

_____

This will help you give out the 'aura' or vibe you want to as you go about your day – and meet potential dates. Note that I don't say 'partner' yet as no-one should rush into a full-on relationship until they've finished with *The Break-Up Survival Kit* and are ready to 'give' without emotional baggage interfering!

☼ Do some role-play with yourself. Imagine someone who seems likeable asking you for a date. Then think how you'd respond – because if you didn't score enough Nos above, then you may well respond by being tongue-tied, negative or even sarcastic. Yes, those who have been hurt often respond to potential dates with sarcasm as a way of deflecting attention from their own insecurities. You know the sort of thing – they sneer at the person who's dared to ask them out, 'ME? Go out with YOU? You've got to be joking!' Well, maybe not that extreme but you get my meaning! Now imagine yourself responding with a straightforward and pleasant answer like, 'Yes, I'd like to meet for coffee one day.' And that's how easy it should be, so practise this!

☼ Lastly, it's time to open up your mind to date possibilities. You may have a big crush on the gorgeous person, with movie-star looks, in the accounts department. But if you're feeling a bit shaky they may simply make you feel even less confident. Or you may think the loud-mouth in administration is so funny at each Christmas party. But would you really want their cutting, scythe-like humour directed at you while you're still wobbly? No! So start with some down-to-earth dates just for coffee – practice runs, if you like. There may be someone you've noticed who seems nice and you should keep your mind open to doing something simple with him or her. Who knows, it's the 'nice' ones who get overlooked but who may be the best long-term bet! Or practise with a friend of the opposite sex. Take them out and do some dating research – ask them for tips. Nothing like ideas from the horse's mouth!

Rescuing sexual desire

Getting to know your own body again

Sometimes we get stuck in a sexual rut. Perhaps you and your ex were together for years and let your sexual relationship slide into a predictable routine. For example, you always made love on a Friday night after a few drinks and a movie – not very satisfactory when it comes to your sexual confidence. Such a rut makes *you* think that your partner thought you weren't worthy of being creative with! A lot of relationships break up over an unsatisfactory sex life. One of you may stray, or leave before straying, but because you want to look for something more exciting. This dull approach to sex can leave you without much interest. So it's time to find out where your sexual desire may be lingering quietly!

Rediscovering your sexual feelings

You and your sexual feelings are unique. What arouses you may not arouse someone else. Where you like to be caressed may be anathema to another. So let's get to know your body – or rather – *you* get to know your own body again!

! First choose a quiet moment when you're not exhausted.
Friday night after a long week, with fresh memories of your
boss shouting and panicky feelings about deadlines still
causing your heart to thump probably isn't best!

! Next, decide where you are most comfortable. Perhaps it's
snuggled up in bed, lazing in a warm bath, or standing in an
invigorating shower.

! Now clear your mind of any negative thoughts. These may
be about your ex – 'They never cared about my pleasure!' –
or negative attitudes you've carried all your life – 'Sex really is
rather dirty!'

! Substitute instead thoughts of something that recently
made you think of sex. Maybe you saw Brad Pitt's or Julia
Roberts' latest film and thought 'She/he's sex on legs!' It may
be that someone caught your eye as you got on with your
day. They were the sort of person who made you think
'Wow!' Whoever or whatever it was – bring that
image/scenario to the forefront of your mind. Enjoy the
moment as you lounge in bed or the bath.

! Now it's time to caress yourself however you like to be
caressed. Recall how you once felt – before the heartache!
There must have been things that felt good and now you
are free to experiment!

! It's so important to you as a whole person that any negative
sexual attitudes, particularly as a result of your relationship
with your ex, should be banished. You as a human being
have a basic right to enjoy your sexual self. Time for an
intimate affirmation here. I'll be really honest and share mine
with you so that you feel positive about creating your own.
After my break-up I reminded myself that, 'Sex is a healthy,
creative pursuit. I can enjoy it again!' Write yours here:

_____

!   And finally, sex is OK – even better than OK. It can be fantastic! But, and this is a big but, you have to be ready and confident when you move on to a sexual relationship with someone new. You need to be in control of the timing of when you go to bed and what you do.

How to tell if you're ready for sex with someone else

Once you've established (through a little fooling around on your own) that you can still get sexually aroused, it's important to decide whether you're ready, or not, for a sexual relationship. This can be an anxiety-ridden time. What's important is that none of the normal worries cloud the issue of how you'd cope going to bed with someone new.

Select either True or False for the following statements:

- I feel confident about expressing my sexual needs – True / False
- Thoughts about 'sex with my ex' are infrequent – True / False
- I feel quite sexy at times – True / False
- When I see a sexy scene in a movie it stirs feelings in me – True / False
- I don't take to heart anything negative my ex said about our sex life during the break-up – True / False
- I couldn't see myself being pressured into bed – True / False

Four or more True answers and you're well on your way to being ready to start a new relationship when you've met the right person. Proceed cautiously if you selected 'False' to either the first or last statement. These are bound up with feelings central to progressing with your Break-Up Survival Kit. You need to feel able to choose when you have sex with someone and to express your needs. Particularly if you had difficulty expressing your needs to your ex!

Sex Siren/God or Sex Shy? What message are you giving off?

Now you're potentially ready for a relationship that includes sex, what about the message you may be giving off to potential lovers? It's important that while you're finding your 'dating feet' you consider how potential dates perceive *you*. Cindy is a good case in point. When I met her she was very upset about being what she termed 'used'. What Cindy wanted more than anything was a new relationship now that she felt she was really over her ex.

Cindy was back on the singles 'market' but didn't think about the message she was giving off. With discussion it became obvious she was giving the message, 'I want to have fun, I'm out for a good time!' Full stop! Her light-hearted approach to men was being misinterpreted as 'easy target'. Whereas Cindy hoped each date would lead to another, the guys were interested in the message she was giving. When they realised she wasn't going to 'give' what they thought, they didn't phone again.

So those signs and signals are important when you've been out of the singles market. Answer the following to see if you need to revise the message you give out:

1) Do you find yourself the centre of attention when you go out?

    A) Sometimes – if I'm feeling super-confident

    B) Yes, the opposite sex seems to flock to me

    C) No, I rarely/never get attention

2) Do you respond to chat-up lines?
   A) Only if the 'giver' seems interesting
   B) Yes, by giving one straight back
   C) They make me tongue-tied

3) Do you feel the opposite sex misreads you?
   A) No, I've not had any misunderstandings
   B) Yes, and sometimes I try to throw them on purpose
   C) I don't really get the chance to find out

4) Do you enjoy telling risqué jokes?
   A) With my friends I might
   B) Yes, they're terrific icebreakers
   C) No, I'd be embarrassed

5) Has anyone ever accused you of being a flirt?
   A) I can flirt but wouldn't do it to upset someone
   B) Yes, and I really don't understand it
   C) No, I've never been accused of that

6) Do you say one thing to a potential partner when you know you mean another?
   A) No, what's the point?
   B) Yes, as I like a bit of a game
   C) No, I tend to let them do the talking

4+ As – Clear messages!
4+ Bs – The sirens are wailing!
4+ Cs – Shy and elusive!

Giving off the right message

Sex siren/God

! Don't give off mixed messages – people don't like the confusion and you could lose out on someone nice.

! Consider the clothes you're wearing. We have the right to wear what we want. But others have the right to interpret our clothes! If you're dressed like a floozy (the girls), or pimp (the boys), people will respond to this by not taking you seriously as dating material.

! Ensure that you chat to members of your own sex too when at social events. If you surround yourself only with members of the opposite sex people may assume you're on the make. (Even if you are, you should be subtle about it!)

! Risqué jokes/crude remarks may be fine with old friends but they give out an 'easy' message when told to strangers.

! Don't sexualise everything you say. For example, if someone comments about something in the news and you're the first to find a way to relate it to sex.

Shy and elusive

! You need to break free a little. Perhaps try on some slightly sexier clothes to put you in the mood for socialising.

! Practise in a mirror shaking off your 'coy' smile for a delicious one.

! Think about the messages that *you* find attractive Then try giving these off yourself. For example, flash a smile at someone you like.

! Run through your mind, during moments of panic, all the reasons why you'd be a good date! Hold these in your mind.

! Practise some things to talk about with a potential date when you're on your own.

If you're giving off clear messages, relax and continue to enjoy yourself when out. You're unlikely to attract the wrong sort of sexual attention. But if you do I'm confident you can cope with it!

The newly single sex checklist

I'd like to finish this chapter with a list of things that'll give you a boost to your sexual confidence. Things to *remember* so that you're *unforgettable*!

☼ Devise your own sexual trademark. Something that you know you do really well. When you do go to bed, drive your new lover crazy with your technique. It may be a kissing or massage technique, but it's all yours.

☼ Give your imagination a work-out! Think through some fantasy scenarios. Relax and enjoy them. One day you can share them with a new love.

☼ Keep some essential oils by your bedside. Ylang-ylang, musk, and lavender all have sensual properties. A few drops sprinkled on your pillow will get you in the mood or you can give your new love a massage with a few drops mixed into a massage oil base.

☼ Stock a 'toy box' in your bedroom. Fill it with anything that can aid erotic pleasures. Some feathers and a kitchen basting brush make great erotic implements when paired with massage oil. You can swirl them through the oil, drizzled on your lover's body. Keep some naughty lingerie in it, too, for a quick change. Also a pot of honey or chocolate spread for making yourself into 'dessert'! Make sure your mood music CD is handy too.

☀ Be prepared to crack a new lover's secret sex code. Listen and learn. As they gasp softly, do more of that! If they guide your hand, make sure you follow eagerly. Then try asking them what they'd like or if what you're doing feels good.

☀ Get a good book on sexual positions. If sex was dull with your ex, reading about new positions will give you loads of ideas for the future.

☀ Never be afraid to instruct! It's the way you do it that counts. In a soft, sensitive voice, ask your new lover to touch and caress you *where* and *how* you like. I can assure you this will turn them on.

Last but not least, you as an adult have a right to enjoy sexual relationships of *your* choice. Don't let anyone tell you, or make you feel, otherwise.

The most important thing I've learned about sex and being single again from this chapter is: _____

_____

And I'm going to remind myself of this!

GETTING EVEN

Without getting in trouble

This chapter is somewhat shorter than the last couple. To be honest, I hope your *Break-Up Survival Kit* will be moving you on to the point that revenge against your ex is NOT the biggest thing on your mind. But I know there will be some of you reading this who have your little hearts set on a bit of revenge. Therefore, I'd rather keep you on the straight and narrow and get you thinking in terms of revenge that won't be damaging. But here's a chapter warning: do not seek revenge of any sort that you know is dangerous, unlawful or blatantly destructive. And do *not* use the more light-hearted methods suggested here, and then come back and complain they got you into trouble. These are suggestions more in the spirit of humour. You are an adult and may choose to do something but that is your choice. *You have been warned!*

I must admit, revenge can be sweet – and it can take many forms. In my own case the best form of 'revenge' has been to embrace life and get on with it – without looking back or worrying about what my ex is up to. Because, quite frankly, whatever the circumstances of people's break-ups, if one or both partners are focussed on revenge it means there's still some sort of connection there – and probably an unhealthy one at that. Also don't forget that in *looking* as if you're trying to get back at your ex, they, and others will assume that your life is fairly shallow at the moment. Otherwise, why would you waste your precious energy on them?

But we all move on differently and rescue our emotions in our unique way. That's why I'm willing to contemplate some of you taking some form of revenge: if it's revenge that won't cause you any regret. Did you read that last sentence carefully? Won't cause *any* regret! That means to you, your ex, or any friends/family that may get involved in the vengeful plans (perhaps without even knowing it!). So let's take a look at some of the acceptable and unacceptable forms of revenge.

Revenge that you won't regret

The best ways to exact revenge that you won't regret usually involve toying with your ex's sense of pride, self-worth and embarrassment. You've been through a break-up – so you know how much your feelings matter! They can be all over the place and even the smallest incident, challenge or remark can lead to self-doubt. But that's why I use the phrase 'toying'. I don't think it's good for *you* to try and do serious damage to someone else's self-esteem even if they are your mean, nasty, horrible ex! Here are some tactics that won't do serious damage:

! Hide and seek! If your ex still hasn't claimed all their belongings hide their most valuable possession. It might be their treasured football pennant that hangs sadly from a wall – and of course it may have been their love of football that appeared to eclipse their love for you and resulted in the break-up! It could be their prized cuddly toy (you know those fairly hideous puppies, etc., with fake sad eyes) that used to annoy you terribly. And you quite enjoy sticking 'Mr. Dog' or 'Happy', or whatever pet name your ex gave it, in a dark cupboard. Once you know they've searched high and low through the belongings they *do* have in their possession, it can mysteriously turn up. Let them sweat for a while and then innocently hand it over. They can never prove that you were gleefully hanging on to it.

! Acting skills! Fine-tune your ability to act happy and radiate contentment. Whenever you go somewhere you will meet people whom you or your ex both knew and you need to act as if the world is at your feet even if inside you're still desperate, depressed and desolate. This information about the happy, radiant you will get back to your ex, I can assure you!

! Juicy gossip! Spread gossip about your gorgeous new love – even if he/she is a figment of your imagination, as you haven't met anyone yet. If people are too discreet to ask if you've started seeing someone, work it into the conversation. Ensure that you give all sorts of details such as your new date being handsome/beautiful, intelligent and successful. But don't over-do it or they may smell a rat. Again, this news will get back to your ex faster than you can say, 'I made it all up!'

! Sex with the ex! When anyone enquires about whether you're missing the 'sexual' side of your relationship, or if 'sex was the last thing to go' in your relationship with your ex (and believe me, people are that nosey!) – make a face like, 'Oh God, he/she was awful!' Or sigh deeply and allude to the 'fact' that those years were the most frustrating of your life. No-one likes to have aspersions cast on their sexual prowess. And if you think that the previous two ideas will get back to your ex, this one will, faster than you can say, 'sex with the ex!'

! Mischievous moments! Everyone has some prized possession that they obsess over and your ex is no different. You could spread a rumour that your ex wants to sell their prized record collection, favourite painting, or their hideous, but treasured, porcelain animal collection! Like 'Chinese Whispers', soon your ex will be deluged with enquiries about how much the items are going for. Very puzzling until they trace the source of the rumours! Or you could spread a rumour that your ex is looking for new love and they are looking for someone like a 'quiet, home-loving, stamp collector'. Soon everyone will be trying to pair your ex off with the likes of their maiden aunt. Not that I have anything against 'quiet, home-loving stamp collectors' or maiden aunts – but you get my point!

! When couples break up many friends find they can't sit on the fence and remain friendly with both of you. Somehow, they've got to do some choosing and end up cutting one of you out of their address book. This is unfortunate but simply human nature. People feel uncomfortable when, e.g., they are pressured to report about one of you to the other – it's easier not to know what both of you are up to. So it's up to you to get hold of the joint address book and schmooze your old crowd. Charm them, spoil them, and make sure they want to keep you in their address book. Not your ex!

! Be an enigma! When you bump into your ex look them straight in the eye with a mysterious look – as if you can see inside their soul! Then allude to the fact that you've heard something about their 'unhappiness'. Keep them guessing – they'll be desperate to know what you've heard, especially since you'll be making it obvious that what was said wasn't positive. This will drive them crazy – they'll not want to beg you for your source of info but they'll be at your mercy.

! Fantastic fantasies! To keep you out of trouble but simply assuage your need to get even, lie back and imagine something awful happening to your ex. Think of your ex suddenly finding that he's impotent with his young, new lover. Or what about your ex bursting her trousers in the middle of a party? If anything, such relatively harmless fantasies will bring a smile to your face. And after all, your *Break-Up Survival Kit* is about finding the happier you again! However, if these fantasies cross over to 'the darker side' and you constantly fantasise about your ex dying a horrible death, or getting a weapon and using it on them, you need to talk to your healthcare professional – and fast! The occasional, fleeting dark thought is OK but repeated obsession with such things is NOT!

Revenge you won't regret

My first and most important piece of advice is DO NOT seek revenge while you are still angry! Remember the saying that 'revenge is a dish best served cold' – that means when you're not still 'hot', i.e., hot-tempered. You may still be hurt or unhappy, but when you are angry you're likely to make choices that no sane person would. Simon is a good example of why you shouldn't take revenge when you're still angry. He was fuming over his ex-girlfriend's seemingly effortless transition from having lived with him to moving on to someone new.

When I met Simon the damage was already done – and he regretted it! Simon had spread a rumour that Liz had given him a sexually transmitted disease – a particularly nasty thing to do. At first it seemed to have the desired effect – Liz and her new boyfriend broke up when the boyfriend got wind of the rumour through the grapevine of mutual friends all three shared. He assumed that Liz wasn't being honest with him. You see, sexually transmitted diseases are a hot topic – and he reacted strongly to the rumour. Liz tried everything to convince him that this wasn't true.

Eventually, Liz's arguments won through and she got back with her new boyfriend, who felt rather ashamed of his initial reaction. All her friends rallied around to investigate where exactly the rumour had started. It didn't take much amateur detective work to trace the gossip-trail back to Simon. He completely lost face and credibility, but more importantly he lost some friends. Simon had also lost potential dates – one woman he asked out a few months after this disaster asked if 'he was the one who spread untrue rumours, and if so she wasn't having anything to do with him!' Eventually Simon got through all this and realised that his anger had made him see 'red' and *not* sense!

The following are things you should NOT be considering:

- **!** Forget food! You may think it's funny to send something like 'off' chocolates or fruit to an ex but nothing that could cause food poisoning is funny! People end up hospitalised and worse from food poisoning.

- **!** Respect the law! If you commit an act that is against the law you deserve to be punished. Vandalising your ex's car is against the law, as is destroying any of their property or cutting up their clothes, throwing paint on possessions, etc. Even things that seem fairly innocent may end up looking like harrassment. Don't advertise their prized possession for sale or put their name and details down with a dating agency advertising for a kinky lover. Just rely on innocuous rumour-spreading, as described above.

- **!** Danger! It's not worth putting yourself into any danger in the pursuit of seeking revenge on your ex.

- **!** Don't humiliate yourself! Many seeking revenge only end up humiliating themselves – like Simon. The world sees that *they* are desperate, depressed and desolate – and it should only be your loved ones, not the uncaring world, that sees you like this. So, running up to your ex in his favourite drinking haunt and throwing a drink/ink/something smelly on his favourite suit will only make you look half-mad. Or how about showing up at their place of work and ranting about how they couldn't please you in bed and had the nerve to run off with someone else? This will make you look *completely* mad when of course your vengeful plan was to jeopardise your ex's career by calling into question their judgement in their boss's eyes.

! Never, ever stalk! Do you remember the character 'Mary Ann' in the sitcom *Cybil*? She was constantly humiliating herself by stalking her ex 'Dr Dick'. People would come across her hiding in bushes, peering in his windows, etc., and it only served to make her look comically pathetic. But in real life laws exist against this sort of behaviour. So if you think following your ex around and not giving them any peace is good revenge – definitely think again!

Ready for Revenge Check list

Select True or False

- I think constantly about my ex having bad luck   True / False
- I find it hard to forgive and forget generally in life   True / False
- I admire those who 'get one back' on people who've harmed them   True / False

- I strongly believe in an 'eye for an eye'   True / False
- The world would be a better place without some people   True / False

Three or more Trues and you're liable to take revenge you regret.

The five main ingredients for revenge without regret:

1) Think before you take any action against your ex.
2) Get a second opinion from a friend/family member whom you respect (preferably for their level-headedness!) before taking any action.
3) Write your plan of action on a piece of paper and re-read it no sooner than 24 hours later. Is it still a good idea?
4) Think through these questions. Is it legal? Is it harmful? Is it truly destructive to your emotional well-being or your ex's?
5) Try to imagine the after-shocks, after the event. Really think through the possibilities. Will you be upsetting an innocent party who just happens to be part of the plan? Like 'hideous Aunt Jane' from the 'party-invite' example above, who actually doesn't deserve humiliation simply because she's a crashing bore and over-opinionated?

And my last piece of advice on this topic is that you will *never* find better revenge than finding your own happiness again and putting two fingers up to your ex!

The most important thing I've learned about revenge against my ex from this chapter is: _____
_____

And I'm going to remind myself of this!

6

THE DIVORCE DIET
The food of love

So, finally we've reached the topic of food – something that is very important to us since we need to eat to live. But where do we go wrong when it comes to the 'food of love'? That is, when *love* goes wrong, why do so many of us use food in inappropriate ways? The answer lies in how central food is to our lives – it's there around us at all times. Also, with society now so obsessed with food you can't help but be reminded in every type of media – TV, films, advertising, magazines, newspapers, the internet, etc. – that food of all types and for every craving (even one of the heart) is at your fingertips.

But, and this is a big and interesting one, it's not that simple, because our 'relationship' with food can be very complex and inextricably linked with our emotions. This is because food links into our whole sense of ourselves as people, especially at the most intimate level of comfort and 'love'. The sensuality of the mouth plays a part in this. When we are 'in love' our mouths are not only used for communication with our lover but also for giving affection and in making love. And this also includes food and its part in 'love play' – when you share romantic meals, feed each other and eat delicacies because they look gorgeous and sexy and are thought to contain aphrodisiac qualities. So food and love are bound up in interesting ways.

It doesn't stop there, since we can trace this intimate relationship with food back even earlier in our lives. Our first intimate bond with 'life' itself originates from our very earliest experiences as babies. Not only did we receive the nourishment necessary for life through our mouths by the breast or bottle, but our first experience of touch at an intimate level came through this 'feeding'. Add together all these important events – from babyhood, through being surrounded by food and food images, to food and our lover, together – and it's obvious why food comes to take such a central place in our lives.

Put in this light it's understandable how negativity and unhappiness after a break-up is not simply reflected in emotional terms but also in physical ways – like our eating habits changing and our weight being affected by this. This will come as no surprise to you, as this far into *The Break-Up Survival Kit* you will be wholly aware of the many types of possible reactions there are to heartbreak. What is interesting to note is that once upon a time it was recognised that relationship breakdown often led to 'physical' changes in appearance, like a new hairstyle or wardrobe, for women who quite literally wanted to 'wash a man right out of their hair'.

Nowadays, with society's obsession with food and our complex relationship with food and love outlined above, it frequently leads to swift and sometimes too great, weight loss or gain. Recent examples in the media of dramatic weight loss include the experience of Vanessa Feltz (mentioned earlier) and Anne Diamond. Previous examples include Liz Taylor, whose weight has yo-yoed across break-ups, Monica Lewinsky with her own weight-loss-and-gain approach to handling the Clinton saga and its aftermath, and Melanie Griffiths after her break-up from Don Johnson.

This brings us to the question of what is the right weight. There are two main ways of looking at this. Firstly, there are the weight charts you find in doctors' offices. These give parameters of weight range related to height that would be considered medically healthy. However, these charts do not take into account individual differences in lifestyle that can have a direct bearing on what would be a healthy weight.

The other way of looking at weight is a more individualistic and psychological approach. A good weight would be one where you felt fit and well and could be as active as your needs require. You'd also be content with your size and so *not* obsessed by your weight. Perhaps the best way to look at weight is a combination of the two. This second way of viewing weight is crucial to accepting yourself and the needs of your lifestyle without being bullied into feeling you're half human if you're not stick-like. And this knowledge should be tempered with a general idea of what the medical guidelines state about height and weight ratios in the Body Mass Index chart.

Can weight change after a break-up ever be 'good'?

But surely, you might ask, some weight loss or gain (depending on the circumstances) is good? The answer quite clearly is 'No!' *unless* that weight change is beneficial for an individual's health and the change has been achieved properly! As well as relationship breakdown there is also a runaway sense of having to lose weight in our society. So, with all this pressure, how can we encourage 'positive' weight change? The main way is first by understanding our emotional responses to a break-up. The next step is to weed out any negative emotional energy in these responses and substitute positive energy. What exactly is this positive energy? It is when sensible weight loss (or gain if that's what suits you and your health) comes about through a sense of *wanting* to do something for yourself, in the *right* way and over the right time. It is weight loss driven by emotional rescue, NOT attention-grabbing, self-loathing, emotional desperation, or a toxic cocktail of those – negative emotions we will be taking a closer look at shortly.

During emotional rescue you are in control of your emotions. They are NOT running away with you, leading you down a dangerous self-destructive path where lack of proper nutrition leads to weight loss through negativity or where indulgence in comfort eating leads to too rapid gain. And these in turn may lead to lack of energy, anxiety, depression and even further inability to fight off illness when coupled with the usual upset of break-up.

Feelings-about-food check list

Please tick the choice – Yes or No – that best represents your feelings about food. Honesty is imperative. Anyway, whom would you be fooling if you weren't honest? You wouldn't be fooling yourself and no-one else is going to see this!

- Thoughts of food cross my mind many times a day (even when I'm not hungry)   Yes / No
- When I'm upset I eat more   Yes / No
- When I'm upset I eat less   Yes / No
- I frequently regret something I've eaten   Yes / No
- I tend to have favourite foods that I then get sick of   Yes / No
- I've been told I'm a 'fussy/faddy' eater   Yes / No
- I'll eat anything put in front of me   Yes / No
- There have been times when I have eaten in secret   Yes / No

- I envy those who seem to eat anything and look good
  Yes / No
- I'm obsessed by my size   Yes / No
- My weight makes me unattractive to a potential partner
  Yes / No
- My ex used to make me feel bad about my size/eating habits
  Yes / No

How to score

There isn't any fancy scoring system to this check list. If you've ticked two or more Yes answers then you need to develop happier feelings inside so that your eating habits are NOT so important. If you only ticked one Yes, but it's any of the last three items, then the same goes for you! Try the following:

Rescue strategy for renewing positive food feelings

Let's begin now to get you feeling happier about the part that food plays in your life.

 Create your own food-affirmation. For example, during my divorce I was so stressed that my appetite decreased a bit too much (obviously for the wrong reason – fear of coping). My affirmation became: 'Relax, breathe deeply, take in the nourishment *you* need for coping with a busy life!' It was as if I was instructing myself – talking as a soothing third person. Write yours here:_____

_____

 Give yourself a few tranquil minutes before mealtimes.
Meditate on your good qualities – and *don't* say you don't

have any! This time will allow you to focus on feeling calm. This is far better than to start a meal stressed and either not be able to eat enough (the problem I had) or stuff in as much as you can to alleviate stressful feelings.

☼ Write down what's most important to you in the aftermath of your break-up. For me it was my children. Take a few moments each day to focus on this. Remind yourself of how this is important whereas food is important only in so far as we nourish ourselves and enjoy what we eat. Note here what's most important to you: _____

☼ Select a photo of yourself from a time you were happy with life – preferably one without your ex in it! Get this copied and pin it up at critical points around your home – on your mirror, the fridge door, your desk, etc. Believe that you will feel like that again!

Dieting

Before we go further on your recipe for rescue in terms of your relationship to food after the break-up, let's take a look at what's already out there. Tons of diets! So, this section is aimed at those of you who are concerned with losing weight rather than the ones who need to put it back on! There are so many diets on the market, ranging from the traditional to the downright weird, and everything in between, that it's got to make you wonder if it's all fluff and no substance!

Here are a few examples I've come across. Some diets state that you shouldn't mix carbohydrates with protein – so you alternate eating those. Others say that you should only eat protein, full stop (plus veggies of course!). Some diets recommend a week on something fruity – like pineapple. Others want you to indulge in something veggie – like carrots. Some say that losing weight is about eating eight times more roughage per day for the rest of your life. Then there are the truly hideous ones that put you on some horrible concoction of mystery liquids for a number of weeks, at which point you're allowed to start adding in normal food. And of course there are diets that say a little of what you fancy is good for you and recommend that you just stick to a balanced regime the rest of the time. These latter seem the most sensible but need to be appreciated with a positive frame of mind. In the end, if eating (whether over or under-eating) is a problem for you, it is still only the symptom of unhappiness after a break-up. Inappropriate use of food either way symbolises what's going on in your heart and mind. It's those overpowering angry, unhappy and anxious emotions that dictate your eating behaviours!

Why are there so many diets? Because of the extremely high failure rates with diets (as people are *only* treating the symptoms – their eating behaviour – and *not* their hearts and minds) there is a constant demand for that new magic cure that will help people lose weight for ever. Many people get locked into a cycle of trying the latest diet, losing some weight and then having the pounds pile back on. This is because they can find the sheer willpower to stick at a diet in the early phases. The prospect of weight loss helps them force the negative emotional issues dictating their *long-term* eating habits under the carpet.

But, once the novelty has worn off and their emotional pain forces it's way back to the surface, the old eating habits resurge as a means of comfort or familiarity. Of course, all dieting isn't bad. Certainly, if your doctor told you that you needed to lose weight for your blood pressure or diabetes, etc., then you should follow that advice. Likewise, if you are feeling lethargic due to excess weight, or due to lack of calories from being too slim, you should also now consider following *The Break-Up Survival Kit* in full. But *in full* means taking the entire contents of this chapter seriously at both the level of your eating habits and, more importantly, the level of your emotional well-being. Of course, you must also follow the recipes for emotional rescue throughout the rest of the book. As soon as you're feeling better about the break-up, your relationship with food will get better! At this point you should check with your own doctor before considering any weight loss/gain plan – even with the nutritional advice offered at the end of this chapter by medical doctor, Doug Spurr MD (who happens to be my brother).

Key message for your dietary rescue! In order to stress how seriously I mean what I say about your relationship with food I want you to hold this key message in your mind from now on: **Only if I am happy inside, moving on positively after my break-up and willing to see how food can be the symptom of unhappiness, am I ready to regain control over my relationship with food.**

And secondly, repeat after me: **Inappropriate use of food is the symptom of emotional unhappiness!** In fact, I think you should write this out here to embed it firmly in your mind:

_____

_____

This is a key message! Until you accept this fact you will not develop a happy, healthy relationship with food.

The negative feelings that prevent a recipe for rescue

So, how is an inappropriate relationship with food a symptom of break-up unhappiness? And what sorts of feelings are reflected during/after relationship breakdown through weight loss or gain?

I believe that weight loss/gain usually reflects four main sets of negative emotions that ALL have the possibility of being channelled into POSITIVE emotions. Here they are:

1) **Attention-grabbing** – Yes, we're going back to those smoke signals! Much weight loss comes down to being symptomatic of a desire to grab an ex's attention, or even to try to win back an ex. The underlying attitude being, 'Just look at me now!' An example in the media is that of Della Bovey when she tried to win Grant back from Anthea Turner. She shrank a couple of dress sizes, partied on the town and initially succeeded with her smoke signals – only to be left again later. And not because of her weight, but as Grant Bovey said in essence, 'There wasn't a proper marriage any more.' Melanie Griffiths evidently fell victim to this too, when she tried to show Don Johnson just how good she was looking when their relationship hit the rocks.

A woman, Anna, who consulted me had tried the same tactic. She was desperate to get her husband Pete back after he left her for someone else. Anna starved herself from a size 16 to a size 10 and tried to flaunt it everywhere she knew Pete would be. On the outside she looked a confident new woman. On the inside she was desperately unhappy. Anna was constantly hungry, started to catch every cold going – and she didn't get Pete back! You see, he hadn't left her because of her size 16. He'd left her because of what he saw as a basic clash of personalities.

After embarking on my *Break-Up Survival Kit* Anna came to see her approach to food, and the break-up generally, as reflecting unhappiness within herself. As Anna became happier and more optimistic over a few months, her weight stabilised at something a bit smaller than her old size 16. She had loads of energy and put that into all sorts of exciting new things – except worrying about her weight! And quite simply she had a lot more energy because her emotions weren't being squandered on battling with her basic need to eat!

I can now hear you all sighing, 'A few months!? Will it take me that long to work through *The Break-Up Survival Kit*?' We'll come to this at the end of the four negative emotional reactions!

2) **Self-loathing** – Self-loathing can relate to either weight loss or gain. Some women react to relationship break-up with extremes of weight loss or gain brought on by the pain of relationship failure. They take this 'failure' so much to heart that it permeates their entire sense of themselves as a person. In some cases the reactions can be so serious as to lead to eating disorders. The underlying attitude the person feels is on the one hand, 'I'm such a terrible person I don't even deserve nourishment!' and on the other, 'I'm so hateful it doesn't matter how many pounds I pile on!'

Ellen was a woman who took her relationship break-up to her very core. Many of us do, but for a limited time as the worst of the pain shifts to something more manageable. Also many of us don't let this pain affect our relationship with food so extremely as to become a real health problem. Ellen was the sort of person who always felt responsible for others. Her ex had problems with alcohol and as well as dealing with her own low self-esteem – she felt that his drinking meant more to him than she did – she also tried to manage his deeply ingrained problems. Now, it's one thing to be supportive to a partner struggling with an addiction but it's another to feel utterly responsible for their problems!

All this had been emotionally damaging and Ellen severely restricted her food intake. She felt she was a failure and worthless – not deserving of nourishment. This problem was caught in time and Ellen didn't have to be admitted as an in-patient for treatment. Instead, with careful, in-depth counselling, she made a good recovery in terms of her emotional well-being, which in turn reflected on her relationship to food.

Ellen is an extreme example. If any of you can identify with her, you need to consult your doctor *immediately* to determine what sort of counselling, or other help, you may need. Many, many more of you will be feeling self-loathing that may lead to some over-indulging in comfort food, or denying yourself enough food to meet all your energy requirements – but not on quite such a serious scale. However, it's still important to consider all the points in this chapter in relation to your own experience – and use all the positive strategies to ensure your own long-term wellbeing.

3) **Emotional desperation** – Sometimes people look back in panic on their failed relationship and think, 'I've got to change or *no-one* will ever want me!' Such people are prone to looking for a readily identifiable 'reason' why their relationship failed. Often the 'reason' they come up with reflects their feelings of low self-worth and so they're vulnerable to an underlying sense of 'I wasn't good enough the way I was!'

Their quick-fix solution is to change their appearance – and often their weight – without much thought about long-term strategies for gaining confidence in themselves as a person and whether or not this is an appropriate 'change-response'. I wonder whether this is the reason for Liz Taylor's lifelong search for a soul mate evident through her many marriages. Was there always a worry in the back of her mind that she needed to shed weight in order to attract someone new? That she had to look like a starlet through dieting so that she wouldn't be on her own? And by doing this she was really punishing herself rather than settling in to a weight that would be natural and healthy for her.

Janet is an example of a woman convinced that she wasn't a very good long-term bet. Because she had two young children and no job, she thought that no-one would ever want to take her *and* the children on. Her ex had been good at re-affirming that lack of belief in herself, being a particularly selfish man. Bill assumed that life would be easier if he had ready access to their children without any new men on the scene, while he happily enjoyed his new single life.

Janet went on a weight-loss plan thinking that at least if she 'looked her best' she stood more chance in the local singles group she was planning to join. Of course 'looking your best' and giving out a positive 'vibe' about yourself are two entirely different things. Sure, Janet may have looked a firm size 14 after losing some weight but the message she gave out was just as desperate as her hungry feelings. She was starving herself of food and self-worth. She just didn't seem to attract anyone – and was not emotionally ready to until the time she was willing to start believing more in her positive qualities!

4) **An emotional cocktail of the above** – Unfortunately, after their break-up some people experience a number of overpowering emotions that have a bearing on their relationship to food and weight. This may mean that as well as seeking their ex's attention with a new shape or size that calls out 'Look – I can be what you want!', they may also be full of self-loathing and desperate about the future. In a candid interview after her dramatic weight loss, television presenter Vanessa Feltz alluded to having a number of different emotions guiding her weight loss. She wanted to send a message to her husband, she felt unhappy about herself and she was worried about the future – 'No one will want me like this!' This may be a very strong emotional cocktail for someone to cope with – and not the best driving force for losing weight. Instead, handling such emotions, growing in your ability to cope with your new life, and accepting yourself makes the best platform from which to decide whether or not you wish to change your weight.

How long your *Break-Up Survival Kit* may take

Let's think about the issue of how long it should take you to achieve the aims of *The Break-Up Survival Kit* and put it in perspective. These are changes for life, not some fad diet. Remember how quickly those fail? They are not for the long-term as they only treat the symp—! (Yes, you fill in the gap.) If you've been in a relationship for five, ten, 20 years or more, how quickly do you expect emotional rescue to take place? And I mean *real* emotional rescue so you don't cart a ton of emotional baggage into your next relationship, jeopardising that as well. And believe me, second marriages have an even higher failure rate than first, largely because people rush into them and make the same mistakes.

First, it will take you time to understand any automatic, knee-jerk emotional responses you have to, for example, seeing your ex with someone new, or hearing about your ex's plans for work/new home/activities with your children/etc., or even hearing your old song. Secondly, it'll then take time to devise your own strategies for handling these responses based on all the suggestions in *The Break-Up Survival Kit*. Then, of course, it takes more time to build the courage to take action in response to changes in your life. So be positive, this is all time that will be well spent and will give you a good basis for relationships for the rest of your life.

Will negative emotional responses dictate your relationship with food?

Circle the statement of these three that best describes you (only one choice!)

1) I'm unhappiest when others *don't* notice how I feel

2) I'm unhappiest when I feel I'm not much of a catch

3) I'm unhappiest when I worry no-one will look after me

Circle the statement of these three that best describes you

4) I fear the future will never bring someone to love me

5) I fear in the future I'll always fail in relationships

6) I fear the future is overwhelming

Circle the statement of these three that best describes you

7) Thoughts of my ex make me feel insecure

8) Thoughts of my ex make me feel totally worthless

9) Thoughts of my ex make me feel very upset

Answers 1, 4 & 7 – Prone to attention-seeking Your answers suggest that you may seek attention after your break-up as a source of validation to your self-esteem. You need to make sure this doesn't spin off into your relationship with food and your weight – so that you don't seek attention through inappropriate weight loss.

Answers 2, 5 & 8 – Prone to self-loathing These choices suggest you may suffer from self-loathing if you don't tackle your unhappy feelings. Such feelings may lead you to either denying yourself proper nourishment, or to simply indulge cravings and seek comfort from food – rather than through more emotionally nurturing sources unconnected to food.

Answers 3, 6, & 9 – Prone to emotional desperation In feeling this way you may be prone to making decisions based on your emotions alone without careful thought and consideration. In moments of despair or desperation you may turn to food for comfort – as a stopgap, or breather, taking your mind off your unhappy feelings. This may become a vicious circle – as you deny or indulge your food whims, you get more worried about being acceptable to a future partner.

A mix of answers – An emotional cocktail of the above! Your answers suggest that your feelings could overwhelm you in many different ways. It's important that you start to understand these and slowly weed out the more positive aspects of your post-break-up life. They are there – perhaps being squeezed out by negative feelings right now! It's important again that you don't allow this mass of feelings to become attached to your relationship with food.

Break-up survival techniques for rescuing your relationship with food:

! **Generate Information:** Keep a food diary including the following points each time you eat *or* deny yourself food:

a) What started you thinking about food? (e.g. Something on the TV, or thoughts of your ex flashing through your mind?)

b) Did you try to stop yourself eating? Why? And what did you do? (e.g. Did you try to talk yourself out of it?)

c) What thoughts crossed your mind as you ate (*if* you did)? (e.g. I'm disgusting! Ooh, this feels/tastes good!)

d) After eating *or* denying yourself food, how did you feel? (e.g. I felt great, horrid, or guilty!)

e) If it was *someone else* eating or denying themselves what would you honestly think? (e.g. I'd think they *shouldn't* treat themselves that way! So my question to you is – *why* do *you*?)

! **Identify:** After a week of keeping your food diary, try to identify two main things. First, what gets you started thinking about food (food trigger points), and second, how you mainly feel. I say 'mainly' as there may be many feelings running through you but it's the primary one you should focus on. Write these here:_____ gets me started thinking about food. I mainly feel:_____ (e.g. sad, mad, bad)

! **Alternatives:** Take this information and think of an alternative to what gets you thinking about food. For example, if you run for 'comforting' snacks when someone mentions your ex, try replacing this with a soothing thought (e.g. I'm really doing fine getting over my ex!) and an alternative activity to eating/thinking about/denying yourself food. For example, keep a creative writing notebook where you jot down ideas for poems or stories. You could do something with your hands, like cleaning out a drawer, or phone a friend to talk about something different. My alternative thought: _____ My alternative action:_____

! **Solutions:** As you get used to thinking of alternatives you'll then begin to be more pro-active generally in your life. You'll find solutions to things before negative feelings and thoughts set in, sending you running for cake or chocolate, or sending you into 'deny' mode where you punish yourself – even your natural hunger!

! **Don't forget** – In rescuing your relationship with food you'll also rescue your relationship with yourself – it works both ways!

Individual ingredients

From the four types of negative feelings that can drive you to having a negative relationship with food, try the following:

! **Attention-grabbing** - Seek the spotlight in ways unrelated to food! If you want and need attention right now, make sure it's for the right things, NOT dramatic, unhealthy weight loss!

! **Self-loathing** – Learn to love yourself! You need to go gently on yourself. Your break-up left you with little regard for yourself so start indulging your whims – not with food but with other feel-good activities you enjoy or company that makes you happy.

! **Emotional desperation** – Re-evaluate what's important in your life! Rather than try and rush into new love, worrying that no-one will ever want you – look at the positives you already have going for you. Enhance these and cherish them. They mean much more than putting your precious energy into a second-rate relationship.

! **An emotional cocktail** – Take steps one at a time. You need to slow down and get to know yourself better so that these conflicting emotions don't overpower and confuse you. Learn to identify and separate out the different aspects of your feelings. Don't act on them immediately. Instead, think through a plan of action!

Rescuing strategies for channelling negative food-related emotions into positive ones

*   Identify the new, other you – not the 'food' you. If you've tended to use food inappropriately to 'smooth' the path of emotional issues you now need to stop identifying yourself in this way. Your core self will not be, for example, 'the person who always punishes myself by withholding the food I need, when I feel low.' Instead your core self will become, 'a person who has great potential!' Your new core self:

    _____

    _____

*   Having identified any *inappropriate* responses to food. you now need to identify *appropriate* responses to your emotions! For example, think of a recent moment when you handled something to do with the aftermath of the break-up positively. Perhaps thoughts of your ex flashed through your mind and you imagined them having a great time with their new lover. But instead of running for a piece of comforting cake, your internal voice said, 'My ex's happiness now has nothing to do with my own. I won't get upset by this image of him/her.' I'd like you to note down at least two appropriate responses you've made recently. And don't be hard on yourself – somewhere you will have done something worth highlighting!

    Appropriate response no. 1:_____

    Appropriate response no. 2:_____

    Now keep this firmly in mind – they prove your *Break-Up Survival Kit is* starting to work!

*   Having identified food trigger points that lead to bingeing or

restriction of food, now it's time to think of emotional trigger points. What really sets you off? It may be when *others* mention your ex. Or maybe emotional trigger points occur when you're on your own and come across a reminder. Make a note of these trigger points so you can prepare for them. My trigger points include:

_____

_____

(List as many trigger points as you have!)

Now can you think of how you can prepare for these triggers? Let's take the example of when someone thinks they're doing you a favour by informing you what your ex is getting up to. You could have something ready to say, e.g., 'I've got no interest in what they're up to, thanks!' Or, 'You know I'd rather talk about . . .' and change the subject. In being prepared you'll get a number of benefits. Mainly, your confidence will grow as you see you can take control of the emotional trigger points that sometimes lead you to inappropriate food use/misuse. Also you'll be giving a message that you're moving on.

! It's important to remember that our sad, bad and mad emotions are there for a reason! They tell us that we need to take some sort of action. Unfortunately, too many people suffering from the 3 Ds of relationship break-up (being depressed, desperate and desolate) listen to their hearts but don't do anything about it. What happens when we do this? Our niggling emotions – sadness, anger, etc., push us towards the kitchen for a little bit of something to make us 'feel better'. Or they make us feel generally unworthy so we deprive ourselves of nourishment in the hope of gaining control over something in our lives – our

weight! Wouldn't it be better if we used some of the strategies in this and other chapters to tackle these emotions head on and separate them from our relationship with food.

Good nutrition

Now that you're well on your way to emotional rescue in terms of understanding how your break-up may affect your relationship to food, it's time to turn to Dr Doug Spurr for some sound nutritional guidance. Unless you have special dietary requirements due to a diagnosed medical condition, the following are guidelines for your general nutritional requirements.

First, let's tackle the weight charts doctors use. These give what's known as the Body Mass Index (BMI), which is the ratio between your weight and height. It's calculated by dividing your weight in kilograms by your height in metres squared. This yields the ratio that tells your doctor whether you are within reasonably healthy weight limits. Your own individual circumstances should also be taken into consideration in deciding whether your BMI is at a healthy level.

Here is a simple BMI table:

Age	Underweight	Healthy	Overweight	Obese
35+	BMI under 19	BMI 19-26	BMI 27-30	BMI 30+
18–34	BMI under 19	BMI 19–24	BMI 25–30	BMI 30+

What you need in your daily diet to ensure your health and help you feel good

Proper nutrition through a balanced diet ensures that you have the energy to meet the requirements of your day. It will also help you battle against unhappy feelings from your break-up as you will be nourished and able to meet challenges. A balanced diet is made up of carbohydrates, fats, and proteins.

Typical carbohydrates are the different types of sugars, e.g., fructose in fruit and lactose in milk; starches found in breads, potatoes and cereals; and the cellulose or dietary fibre from fruits and vegetables. Typical fats are found in both plants, e.g., oils like olive and corn oil, and animals – the meats we eat. Proteins are found in a variety of foods like milk, eggs and meats as well as in rice, peas and beans. A balanced diet is a *varied* diet!

Women's dietary requirements: A woman should take in about 2000 calories a day (nowadays you'll see calories converted into kilojoules but most of us still relate to the old-fashioned calorie) with no more than 70 grams of fat. This is based on an average person who is active and takes moderate exercise. It should be noted that recently there has been a trend to lower fat allocations to 45 grams a day. On a 2000 calorie per day diet that would mean about 20% of those calories (400 calories) should be from fat. However, aiming for between 45 and 70 grams of fat is fine.

It is recommended that women eat daily from the main food groups:

1) Five portions of fruit and vegetables. Fruits and vegetables can accompany the three main meals and provide two snacks.
2) Four portions of carbohydrates. In three main meals this may typically be provided through toast or cereals at breakfast, bread or pasta at lunch, and pasta or potatoes at dinner, as well as one snack, for example a cereal bar perhaps accompanied by a piece of fruit (above).
3) Two portions of protein in three meals per day. Typical protein portions are one medium or two small pieces of skinless chicken,

one medium-size lean chop (cut the big piece of fat off pork chops!), a 3 oz (85 g) piece of beef, 60 to 120 grams of fish, 30 to 60 grams of cheese, or one whole egg. Ideally you should not eat beef, lamb, pork, or eggs more than twice a week. Poultry or fish should be limited to no more than five portions per week. It is always better to grill meats and to poach eggs than to fry them.

Men's dietary requirements: A man should take in about 2500 calories per day with no more than 95 grams of fat. This is also based on an average for a man who is active and takes moderate exercise. Again it should be noted that there is a recent trend to lower this level to 56 grams of fat per day for men. As above, aiming for between these two levels is fine. It is recommended that, from the main food groups, men eat the same daily portions of fruit and vegetables, proteins, and carbohydrates, but in larger portions.

Weight loss is best achieved when you are feeling positive in yourself and you simply cut down by about 3–400 calories per day. This can be done by cutting down on fatty foods (e.g. by boiling or steaming vegetables rather than frying them). Taking smaller portions generally at mealtimes will help. Following these guidelines, the average person should lose about one kilo per week. It does *not* mean rigorously reducing your calorie intake. Again, *consult your doctor* before embarking on any weight loss plan.

If, on the other hand, you've been restricting your food intake *too much* due to stress and negative emotions and you know you're underweight, you need to aim to increase your calorie intake. This should be done by having a varied diet – not by eating high fat foods for a quick weight increase.

Exercise and weight

Don't forget the importance of exercise in keeping you fit and energetic. Think through this three-step principle:

1) You **take in** energy in the form of food.
2) Then you **give out** energy through the use of your muscles.
3) Any **excess** energy you've taken in will be stored as **fat**. The happier and more positive you are, the less likely you'll be to take in excess energy in the form of excess food. Likewise, you'll feel less likely to deny yourself unnecessarily.

If you've neglected this part of your life consult your doctor before embarking on new exercise. You should aim for at least four sessions of 20 minutes each per week of aerobic exercise. Aerobic exercise is any exercise that increases your heart rate. Good examples are swimming, brisk walking, cycling and jogging. You should also ensure that you stretch during the week, ideally for ten minutes per day. Stretching keeps your joints mobile and protects your muscles from injury. Stretching should be gentle, without bouncing, and done with a secure position or footing. Yoga classes are ideal for learning to stretch properly and as a start to a new exercise programme. Exercise and stretching not only generally ensure that your muscles and bones stay strong and flexible, but also improve your heart rate and circulation leading to the release of endorphins – the so-called 'feel-good hormones'.

What else you're allowed

Thanks to Dr Doug for that nutritional guidance! Now I'd like to add the following:

- Allow yourself a daily treat – food can be fun too! Simply bear in mind the portions – two chocolates is a fine treat, a whole box is comfort bingeing!

- Break cycles of eating when you're not hungry. Do something else with your hands!

- Food is not an evil – you should enjoy it. Be as creative as possible in planning meals. Try some of the new exotic fruits and vegetables that are available in stores today. Or try a new combination of ingredients on a basic pasta or rice dish. You can add practically anything to these!

- You are allowed to slip up! So you find yourself in a real bind and you go for some comfort eating, or deny yourself a meal as a form of punishment. What should you do – feel guilty? Yes! You see, feeling guilty is a good thing if you *act* on it! Tell yourself, 'I didn't treat myself very well. I ate/withheld food that I didn't/did need and I felt bad about it. Next time, I'll recognise my emotional trigger that causes that!'

I hope this chapter has been helpful to any of you who have been using food inappropriately in the aftermath of your break-up – either bingeing for 'comfort' or restricting intake as a 'punishment'. And even those of you who have not lost or gained weight inappropriately may have gathered some important 'ingredients' for your recipes for emotional rescue. Now it's time to move on and see whether or not you're *really* beginning to get over your ex!

The most important thing I've learned from this chapter about my relationship with food after my break-up is:

_____

_____

And I'm going to remind myself of this!

HOW HUNG UP ARE YOU ON YOUR EX?

We've now come a long way in *The Break-Up Survival Kit*, covering lots of important topics for the newly single. This means it's time to have a careful think about how much has been sinking in and how far along you are in getting over your ex! It's easy to fool yourself that you're healing at an emotional level. And I bet a lot of you are already eyeing up someone new, thinking you're ready to dive into the dating pool again! But if your heart's really not in it or hasn't healed, you may get demoralised when you do a little dating and actually feel confused, anxious and self-doubting about what you *expect* to be fun.

The stages of emotional rescue

Before we go on to see how far along you've got in your healing process I'd like to outline the stages of emotional rescue. These are the stages through which you pass and 'rescue' yourself from remaining stuck with anger, anxiety or hurt over your ex. I find these quite helpful as a guide to how far you are in this whole process. The six stages are as follows:

Stage One: Realisation - This first stage consists of the dawning, in your *core* self, that your relationship *really* is over. This goes right to your very heart. It may be a swift or slow dawning but once the moment arrives, all sorts of issues are stirred up. These include things like, 'Whoops! How could it have gone this far?' Or, 'This seems unbelievable – we really are finished!' You may have been thinking about breaking up for a long time but, when the crunch comes, life seems to take on a surreal quality.

Emotional content – This stage is characterised by a prevalent feeling of disbelief that can have a numbing effect on you. You can't quite take it in even if *you've* chosen to end the relationship (you're the dumper!). You realise that there's no going back. You may even feel slightly detached from reality as your mind switches into automatic pilot to get you through each day. You may experience lots of doubt about your decision but some part of you keeps heading in this direction.

Stage Two: Devastation – This is when the stress of the situation kicks in and your numbness starts to melt away. That numbness in stage one was very protective in certain ways. You're left with the devastating truth that your life is going to change completely. I say 'devastating' because that's what it feels like at the moment. But think back to Chapter Three and how much you can adapt to change, and you will soon find change less daunting – this stage does not last forever.

☼ **Emotional content** – This stage is characterised by a fast turnover in strong emotions. At times you may feel inconsolable. At other times you may be extremely angry with your ex, with yourself and even the cat! You may experience the three Ds at this time – desperation, depression, and desolation. You may be very concerned about thoughts like 'No-one else will ever want me!' (Even though it's way too early to be thinking of the next relationship!)

Stage Three: Plateau – You now probably realise that the earth isn't going to spin out of orbit, you will survive and every day isn't awful. You still have bad days but somehow they're more manageable. They are manageable because you are devising coping strategies as you learn to break old habits. For example, on the practical side you always expected your ex to fix anything that needed mending and now you're teaching yourself to cope with these challenges. On the emotional side you dreaded each morning, fearing you wouldn't have the strength to face another day but actually you now catch yourself hopping out of bed *some* mornings.

☼ **Emotional content** – You may still experience strong emotions at this stage but you're beginning to feel as though you're coping – they won't overwhelm you. Gloria Gaynor's song 'I Will Survive!' is probably your own internal anthem. You fight hard the urge to slip back a stage. You know that you're recovering but you could so easily slip back into the three Ds if you didn't put in to practice the sorts of positive strategies I've recommended in the previous chapters.

Stage Four: Adaption – This really is a turning point. You start to wake up without anxiety. You're actually enjoying many aspects of your new life. You can still remember the pain you've experienced but you can refocus your mind when it goes back to the dark times. Friends will notice that you discuss your ex less. You need to be aware, however, that any major news about your ex can still rock your world. For example, if you hear that they're very happy with someone new in their life. It still hurts but you'll cope.

☼ **Emotional content** – This stage is characterised by feelings of optimism in many areas. You know you've survived the worst. But, even better, you actually feel quite happy about the things you've accomplished. You may still feel nervous or untrusting about letting someone new into your life but it's much more of a possibility!

Stage Five: Acceptance - Your feelings for your ex are much, much weaker (whatever they originally were – loathing becomes disdain, jealousy becomes disinterest, etc.). You have little time for hate or thinking about revenge. In fact by now you're probably finding some humour in memories of the break-up or your thoughts about what the relationship was like. You really are rising to the challenges of change.

☼ **Emotional content** – This stage is characterised by feelings of excitement over your successes. Also, thinking of meeting someone new feels like a real possibility – it's not frightening or daunting any more but something you'd really like to happen. Or you may feel you've really adapted to single life and want to enjoy it rather than rushing into a new relationship! I reached this stage about 18 months after my divorce. And four months into *really* enjoying the single phase of my life I was introduced to the man who became my second husband. Two messages come to mind – when you're at your happiest you attract worthy partners (my second husband is a fantastic man!) and being single can be great (I was really having a good time doing *what* I wanted, *when* I wanted – and you can too!)

Stage Six: Encompassing healing and hope – When you can think of your ex in perspective, not tarnished by strong feelings (bitterness, vengeful thoughts, deep sadness, etc.) and recognise your own part in the relationship break-up you have entered this phase. Everyone can learn from relationship breakdown! No matter what is wrong or right, or who is 'sinned against' or 'sinner', there are lessons in every relationship. One big lesson I learned was to be more self-reliant in relationships. Two people CANNOT become one! Instead, you need to respect what each of you can contribute to the whole relationship – which is greater than the sum of the two parts! In principle, I always knew this. But applying such principles to oneself is another matter – a matter of learning and growing.

☼ **Emotional content** – There is such joy that comes from gaining confidence in yourself – in your own decisions and intuition – that it's almost tangible. You can feel this stage as it unfolds. It's terribly exciting to develop as an individual and know that you're striving to do your best. Whether you've met someone new during this stage or are single, if you've coped, changed, grown, and learnt, you feel incredibly rewarded.

☼ **An important point to remember:** These stages may last for a few days, weeks, months, or years (if any of the first three stages lasts years, you should be seeking professional help to resolve problems regarding 'moving on'). You may find that you can slip back into the last stage, and pull yourself forward again. You may also find that stages one and two are reversed in your experience. You're an individual and you'll experience the stages of break-up differently!

Where are you in this process?

Think carefully before answering the following and be **absolutely honest!**

Part A – The Ex-Factor – Let's begin with this simple exercise: Keep a brief record for a day of your thoughts. Simply divide a piece of paper in two columns. Label one column 'happy thoughts' and the other 'unhappy thoughts'. Make a tick in the appropriate column each time a thought pops into your mind – whether happy or unhappy. Then count them up at the end of the day.

Score 0 for more happy thoughts than sad. **Score 1** for equal numbers. **Score 2** for more sad thoughts than happy.

My Ex-Factor score for Part A = _____ (0, 1, or 2)

Part B – Ex-Facts - Choose the answers that **best** describe your feelings at the moment.

* I feel more scared than confident about my future True / False
* My bad days outweigh my good days   True / False
* I'm not coping well with changes I've had to make True / False
* My ex got off 'easier' in the break-up than I did   True / False

My Ex-Facts score for Part B = Number of 'True' answers:_____ (0, 1, 2, 3 or 4)

NOW add your Part A and Part B scores: Total score = _____

The following are indicators of where you might be in the six stages of emotional rescue

Your Total Score	Likely Stage
0–1	Stage Six – Encompassing healing and hope
2	Stage Five – Acceptance
3	Stage Four – Adaption
4	Stage Three – Plateau
5	Stage Two – Devastation
6	Stage One – Realisation

Think about your result from the table. Look back at the stage it indicates you're in. Does the description of that stage reflect how you're feeling? Do you think you've been in that stage a while? Is this time justified? These questions should give you food for thought. Perhaps if you're not comfortable with your answers you need to apply more of the strategies outlined in the preceding chapters!

It's not always the case that when you find yourself stuck in one of the stages of emotional rescue it's really because you miss your ex so much. Sometimes other influences keep us stuck. For example, you may be someone who has always found it hard to adapt to change whether in your personal or work life. Adapting to the change brought on by a break-up has been a slow process for you. Or you may be someone who is prone to anxiety and when something sets you back your anxiety works overtime, preventing you from taking appropriate action in your life. These are important considerations. However, let's see how far you may still be stuck because of feelings for your ex holding you back by taking this quiz.

The ex-affect quiz

1) Do you compare potential partners to your ex? Yes / No
2) When you've received good news/done something special do you automatically think, 'I've got to tell . . . (your ex)' Yes / No

3) Do you still try to get information about your ex from friends/family/colleagues? Yes / No

4) Would your 'blood boil/feel depressed/want to die' if you saw your ex with someone new? Yes / No

5) Do you go over and over in your mind different events that took place with your ex? Yes / No

6) Do you find yourself wishing things had worked out differently? Yes / No

7) Do you still have some of your ex's things around when really they should be given back/thrown out/put away? Yes / No

8) Do you ever try to be where you know your ex might be (hoping your paths may cross)? Yes / No

9) Do you dwell on revenge? Yes / No

1 or 2 Yes answers – You're really moving on in terms of your ex, who no longer has much effect on you. You're probably at stage five or six of emotional rescue.

3 to 5 Yes answers – You may be beginning to move on, or you've got stuck depending on how long you've been feeling this way. You're probably at stages three or four of emotional rescue. It could be useful to follow the advice below.

6 to 9 Yes answers – You're still hung up on your ex! Your ex affects you far too much and you're undoubtedly still in stages one or two of emotional rescue.

Some techniques to move you on if you had 3 to 9 Yes answers

- **Thought-stopping** – The things you *think* influence the way you *feel* - I can't impress this upon you enough! Work on changing or stopping your thoughts, and you'll start to feel more in control of your emotions. When unhappy or angry thoughts come into your mind about your ex or the break-up, close your eyes and visualise your hand raising as if to say

'STOP!' Literally form a barrier around the negative thoughts.
Visualise this barrier – it will *contain* those thoughts. Next,
substitute a more pleasant/inspiring thought. For example,
'I don't need to think about my ex, I can think about

_____!'

(Fill in the gap and start thinking about that subject!)

- **Reminders** – Give away reminders of your ex that bring up
  particularly painful memories. Don't cheat – stashing some
  photos in a cupboard where you know you'll find them
  again doesn't count. You've got to be strict. If for some
  reason you wish to keep certain mementos but seeing them
  disturbs you, box them up and have a trusted family
  member/friend look after them.

- **Enlist help from others** – Ask your friends and family to stop
  you in your tracks if you bring up your ex or the break-up.
  Sometimes we allow bad break-up habits to start. For
  example, we start droning on about our ex without even
  really thinking about it. If our friends and family are given the
  permission to remind us when our conversation drifts to our
  ex it can help break such bad habits.

- **Have fun with your friends** – Don't forget that it's far more
  destructive to rush into another relationship than to simply
  enjoy your friends. Do some things you've always wanted to
  – and invite your friends to do it with you. The stronger you
  make these bonds, the more you'll realise you don't have to
  waste time over your ex.

- **Your new attitude to your ex** – Time to develop an 'I don't
  care attitude' to your ex. Even if deep inside you do care, the
  more you try and develop your belief in yourself the more it
  will take hold and work. Visualise all the annoying things
  they used to do. If you need to go back to Chapter One and
  the Ex-Factor Check List for a reminder – do that! And get

even more detailed. Think of how irritating they could be, perhaps around your parents, or their snoring – whatever. Because we can all be irritating – even you and me! When something has cropped up that's thrown you emotionally backwards, telling yourself that you don't care and thinking about these irritations will help.

- **Don't indulge your misery** – If you've moved past stages one and two it's time to stop allowing yourself 'heartbreak time' – when you've been allowed to focus your attention for 15 minutes a day on your ex. Now's the time to start switching off 'your old song' when it comes on the radio – instead of allowing yourself a flood of tears. It's time to stop gazing at your ex's photo while you cry yourself to sleep. Visualise yourself as a big soppy, blubbering wreck – do you really want to give your ex that much power?

- **Stay away!** – When the temptation to seek out your ex feels overwhelming – either to ring them, visit them, or simply hang around where you know they'll be – resist! This is when you need a crisis buddy – the person you trust the most to help you through weak moments. Ring or visit them instead. Don't humiliate yourself by trailing after your ex when the temptation is great. Those feelings will pass and you'll feel much better if you haven't given in to them.

Now you should have a really good idea where you are in the stages of emotional rescue, and how much of a hold your ex still has on your heart. Use this information and you'll be able to use the final chapter to improve your whole life.

The most important thing I've learned from this chapter about how hung up I really am about my ex is:

_____

_____

And I'm going to remind myself of this!

ME? I USED TO LOVE HIM/HER?
Moving on for keeps

By now you'll have learned a lot about your break-up and feelings towards your ex. You only need to look at the end of each chapter where you'll have filled in your final thoughts for a quick refresher of all these areas. So, what I'm going to do as far as possible in this chapter is to avoid discussing your ex! You're going to read about your new attitude, your new life – that doesn't involve *that person*! This chapter will show you how much you can focus on without your ex. This is a very important step even if you're in the early stages of emotional rescue. If you are still *back there* – in the early stages – it will show you the light at the end of the tunnel.

Reading the signs of interest

Let's begin with new relationships because I'm going to assume that since you're reading a book about break-ups, relationships *are* important to you. Now I've been harping on, throughout *The Break-Up Survival Kit*, about *not* rushing into a new relationship and *not* dating when you're not ready. But, by now, many of you will be ready. And for those of you who aren't – but are still insistent on searching for someone new – then at least I'd like to give you the best possible start! A good starting place when you're back on the singles market is to explore the issue of how to tell if someone's interested – and also to think about the messages you may be giving off without even knowing it. A little understanding of body language – the body language of love – goes a long way.

The body language of love

There are so many aspects of body language that I could discuss with you that it would fill an entire book. You, and every other person, give out a whole package of subtle signs and signals – like one big, gift-wrapped, romantic present. People will either untie those ribbons and peel back the paper slowly and carefully, to read your signals and reveal the real you. Or they might rip through the wrap like a child on Christmas morning and actually miss the beauty of the whole package. I don't want you to miss out (and behave like an over-excited child!) so I'm going to list some of the more obvious signs and signals to look for. It's time to shake off old romantic habits that may blinker you to these subtle messages people give out. We need to open your eyes to the very important non-verbal signs to look out for in potential partners.

Lack of attraction – If someone's NOT interested you'll notice the following things and then won't waste your precious time:

♥ Scraping back the hair with the full hand during conversation (different than 'flicking' – see next section) signals discomfort. It means this person is getting nervous – they don't like where this is going.

♥ Clasping the hands behind the head, when answering your

questions, again signals severe discomfort with the topic of conversation. They want to avoid whatever it is and such big gestures give them 'thinking' time. So they only give away what they want by pausing this way and planning what they'll say next.

♥ Looking around during your conversation rather than focusing on *you* signals that they're not interested. They are quite literally looking for a 'getaway' from the situation – even if they can't leave until the date is over. It can also signal lack of interest in the topic of conversation.

♥ Vocal tones that lack emotion and sound matter-of-fact. They are not very happy about continuing with the encounter and with this non-committal tone of voice they subconsciously hope to cut it short. You simply aren't attracting their interest.

♥ Their body turned away from you during conversation quite literally signals that they're ready to get up and walk out the door. At a subconscious level they're trying to get away from you. At a more subtle level, if their feet are turned away but their body is turned towards you, it means they're undecided about their attraction to you.

An important point to remember

Someone may give off all the signs above, but you find they still seem to hang around. Beware if this happens – they may not be bothered about you as a person but still be interested in having sex with you! They may be one of those romantically lazy people who know they don't want a relationship but they've seen your initial interest and then think, 'Why not get what I can from this person?' Don't give it to them!

Attraction – Now we've got some of the negative signals out of the way – let's be positive! What signs should you look for to see if they're attracted by your amazing, magnetic personality?

♥ Dilated pupils and eyes focusing on you for longer than the usual couple of seconds shows distinct attraction to you.

♥ During more intimate conversation, a slight downwards tilt of the head, with the eyes looking upwards through the eyelashes at you, signals an interest in flirting with you. At least, they're testing the water!

♥ Flicking back the hair with a quick, flirty gesture says 'Look at me – I want you to!' When a woman simply fiddles with her hair she's inviting more attention from a man.

♥ Drawing the fingertips over the neck during conversation sends the message that they'd like to get to know you more. In a woman it draws the eyes nearer to her breasts and in a man it draws them to his big-muscled (he hopes!) chest.

♥ Throwing back the head when laughing at your jokes or stories says they're really enjoying your company. They're letting go and feel good with you.

♥ Feet and body pointed towards you shows outward interest. Upper body twisted to you, but lower body twisted away signals they're interested but will play hard to get!

♥ 'Body mirroring' – where you both gently move back and forth with each other in 'tune' with your conversation – suggests a real connection and attraction.

♥ Gentle touching of your forearm or knee during conversation (see below under 'what to do on first dates') signals that they want to draw you into their personal space.

An important point to remember

Someone may give off all these signals and be genuinely attracted to you but you still have to respect the pace they want to move at. For example, it's become obvious they're attracted to you but that doesn't mean they want to jump into bed with you!

Once you've found someone new

Once you've met someone and read their initial signs of interest let's tackle the first date. This can really raise your anxiety. Even if your ex was a three-eyed monster with horns, you were still used to their little ways. It's important to put your best foot forward with any new candidates for the position of your new boyfriend or girlfriend! Bear in mind the following on first dates:

Five things you definitely should not do on a first date!

1) Don't discuss your ex or go on about what your 'perfect partner' would be like.
2) Don't drone on about how horrible life is. Such a negative attitude is repellent!
3) Don't be too eager. For example, don't be free the very next day if they suggest a second date. A clingy, over-eager attitude is a turn-off.
4) Don't be indecisive. When asked where you'd like to go on the date, or what you'd like to eat in a restaurant – speak your mind, make choices, and give an opinion. When you say things like, 'I don't know,' or 'Let's do what you want to,' it sounds either you can't be bothered or as if you're boring because you don't have a mind of your own!

5) Don't eye up other 'talent' (i.e. *ignore* anyone gorgeous who happens to walk in where you and your date are), make suggestive remarks, or go on about how 'sexy' Brad Pitt is (or Julia Roberts if you're a guy!). These remarks are fine in casual company but make you look easy (if you're a woman) or sleazy (if you're a man).

Five things you definitely should do on a first date

1) Definitely hold their eye contact a little longer than usual. This shows that you really are interested in them.
2) Flirt! Giggle, laugh, gently tease, use a lighter, softer tone of voice (if you're a woman), and a slightly lower, relaxed tone of voice (if you're a man).
3) Be happy to volunteer the 'positives' in your life. If you're really enjoying a new evening class, or learning how to salsa dance – talk about it. It's very attractive to watch someone's face light up when they talk about the things they enjoy.
4) Ask questions! Be interested and willing to learn about this new person. Everyone has their own story, so give them a chance to tell it.
5) Enter their personal space, if you really like them, with small, gentle taps on their arm or knee as they're telling you something. This melds those two invisible – but still existent – personal spaces together.

Making the first move!

A few of you may be thinking, 'I don't need instructions in this area!' But most of you, if you're honest, will be thinking, 'Oooh! This is scary territory!' Such critical points in a fledgling relationship make you feel flustered even thinking about them. So let's tackle the moment that has provided many comic scenes in film and on TV where noses bang together, one person draws away in disgust, or the person keeps trying but events conspire to keep their lips from kissing! You've just come out of a long relationship, you've had your first date or two and you're dying to kiss this new person goodnight. You haven't kissed anyone else, except your ex, for perhaps ten years. You don't want to be rejected – but how can you get that kiss in to show you're attracted? There are two ways:

I) **Orchestrate it:** You can manoeuvre things so that *they* make the move to kiss you. As your date draws to a close, move nearer to them, look into their eyes and tell them how much you enjoyed it. Give them time to get the confidence to kiss you! If it doesn't happen, take a pause, then dip your head slightly, looking up at them from under your eyelashes. Think of something specific to say about the date and start again by looking up at them, being near and almost offering your lips. If they don't kiss you they're either shyer than you or not interested!

2) **Do it yourself:** If this new person has been drawing nearer to you, flirting and being positive on the date, then gently lean forward to kiss them. If they start to draw away, stop immediately! They may simply not be ready. You can also try the direct approach and say something simple like, 'I've had such a great time a goodnight kiss would make it perfect!' Either way, done tactfully, and *not* with pressure, they'll either love it or let you know they don't want you to carry on with that first 'move'. You may think I'm being over-cautious about such issues. But, remember, if your 'ex relationship' lasted for ten years or longer, things have changed. A lot of people are very 'forward' but many others are very assertive about their personal space – you've got to respect this!

How to tell if you're feeling love or lust!

When you've come out of a serious relationship and emotions have been riding high, you can't always gauge your own feelings when you meet someone new. (Which is the very reason why I say not to rush into something new! But some of you won't listen, will you?). Circle the answer that best suits you to help you gauge whether it might be a 'love thing' or a 'lust thing' with this new person.

1) Do you always end up in a clinch when together?
    Yes – we spend all our time kissing/cuddling/jumping into bed
    No – we do lots of different things
2) Do you find it hard to judge what they're thinking?
    Yes – I haven't a clue
    No – I think I've got a good idea what they're thinking
3) Do you feel panicky if conversation dries up?
    Yes – I hate that
    No – I feel quite confident we'll soon be chatting
4) Would you drop everything if they ring at the last minute?
    Yes – I'd feel I have to change plans
    No – I'd only do something at the last minute if I was free
5) Does the relationship feel like a whirlwind, out of control, as if you're on a knife-edge?
    Yes – it does
    No – it doesn't

3 to 5 Yes answers: It's probably a lust thing! We all get strong and passionate feelings if we're attracted to the new person in our life. But we don't let them dominate everything we do if we share other things too, and can keep a balance on the situation! Follow the advice below if you want to try to turn this around. But it is possible

that you *only* want a lust thing with no strings attached right now!
2 Yes answers: You're hovering between love and lust. If you want it to last then you'll have to start doing things outside your home – so you don't end up in the bedroom! Build other activities on even the smallest shared interests to keep busy. Talk about a variety of topics – not just how much you fancy each other or how great it was in bed recently. Don't be swayed to change plans for your new 'love'. If they really care for you (and are not just lusting after you) then they'll understand if you're not free. If you don't know what they're thinking then say what's on *your* mind and try to coax them into conversation.

Only 1 Yes answer: Sounds as if it might be love. You *don't* just fall into each other's arms. You *do* have a life outside this person. And you are getting to know the whole them – not just their sexual side!

How to stop making the same old mistakes

Perhaps you've met someone you really like and you seem to be heading for some sort of relationship. How do you avoid the pitfalls of your last relationship? Every relationship has problems and in terms of your development as a person it's good to learn from them. If the break-up was particularly painful, at least by the time you get to stages five (Acceptance) or six (Encompassing healing and hope) of Emotional Rescue, you can assure yourself you've learned something. Here are a few strategies to use to try and improve your next relationship and all future ones. They largely involve gaining self-knowledge through identifying your typical patterns of behaviour.

- **Identify your expectations:** What do you *really* expect from a relationship? These may be expectations that you keep to yourself but which do influence you. Do you expect a partnership where you are completely equal? Or, would you consider yourself as very independent and needing lots of space in a relationship? Your expectations are crucial to the success of your relationships. If you meet someone with the opposite expectations but hope with time that you can mould theirs to your own – you're probably mistaken! Acknowledge yours honestly then look at potential partners' expectations. Is there room for compromise or are you two really coming from separate corners – and likely to end up in a romantic 'punch-up' **My biggest romantic expectation is:**

  _____

- **Identify the way you tend to react in relationships:** We are all guilty of knee-jerk reactions particularly when it comes to intimate relationships. You know the sorts of things I mean. Do you fly off the handle over certain things? Do you sulk when things aren't done your way? Do certain issues turn you into a 'moaner'? We all tend to have knee-jerk reactions. I used to see red when my ex wouldn't ring when he was going to be late. Instead, it would've been a lot better for *me* to get on with my own things as he was a hopeless case at being on time or keeping people informed. The relationship would never have worked so why raise my own blood pressure over his lack of reliability? Towards the end I did simply deal with my knee-jerk reaction by letting go and not fretting about his time of arrival. **My knee jerk reactions include: _____**
  A solution might be: _____

- **Identify the way you tend to *function* in relationships:**
  This taps into a different level of your relationships from
  the specific ones above. Functioning is broader: it is the
  general attitude or emotional style you bring to your
  relationships. For example, you may be very needy and
  dependent. Or you may be very controlling and
  domineering. On the other hand, you may be
  unpredictable on purpose to throw partners off guard
  because inside you are afraid of them getting to know the
  real you. If your last relationship was very unhappy you
  may need to think whether your functioning is too extreme
  one way or another. You may need to adapt and be more
  flexible – without compromising your basic expectations
  of respect, honesty, etc., in a relationship. **My relationship
  functioning could be summed up in three words:**
  _____ _____ _____ **(be honest!)**
  I could be more flexible by: _____
  (e.g. listening to my next partner more)

- **Honest appraisal of potential partners:** If you can learn to
  be honest about your expectations, basic behaviour and
  functioning in relationships, your next step is to start
  honestly appraising potential partners. Look at their initial
  reactions to you (the body language of love) and then watch
  how they treat you. For example, do they ring when they say
  they will? Do they make you feel good when together, or do
  they make you feel uncomfortable? Do they pressure you to
  do things you don't want (e.g. to stay out later then you'd
  like, to miss work, to go to bed with them, to take drugs or
  drink more than you would). Do they get on with your
  friends and family? Or do they resent sharing your time? The
  more honest you can be about these things the easier it will

be for you to put your foot down or to choose not to continue seeing someone. **Think about past relationships and make a note of any area you have to be aware of here:**

_____

Children and relationship breakdown

If you have children you'll probably have focussed on them more than on yourself during the period of your break-up. There are a few things to bear in mind for those of you with children:

- Keep yourself open to them. Just because you're scared of the questions they might ask, don't shut down in the hopes of avoiding difficult moments. If your child sees that they can rely on you to be open, they'll feel more secure.

- Always give age-appropriate information about the break-up, new arrangements, etc. What you might tell your eight-year-old, you wouldn't your three-year-old.

- All children react differently. So, if you have more than one child, each may take the break-up in its own unique way.

- Always check with them that they're OK. Too many parents decide to ignore the subject if their children seem 'fine'. However, this makes it harder for the child to reach out to you in times of insecurity.

- Always tell your child how much you love them and will be there for them.

- Immediately knock on the head any notion your child has that they caused the break-up. Children are prone to guilt, so ensure that they know they have nothing to do with it.

- Don't criticise your ex directly to your children. Even if your ex is a complete loser as a parent, the children must make up their own minds. Being negative will jeopardise any chance they have of maintaining a relationship with your ex.

- Introduce new partners only when you're secure in the new relationship. Turning your front door into a revolving door of new faces will cause great unhappiness for your children.

- Take care to be fair when a new partner comes on the scene. Don't let all your attentions focus on them as your children will become quickly alienated.

Be gentle on yourself – you're allowed to

A lot of *The Break-Up Survival Kit* has been aimed at lifting your spirits and helping you see the lighter side of the break-up. You will have plenty of reminders of the down side – I don't need to give you that. That said, I do take your pain very seriously. After all, I've been there too. It's really unpleasant feeling like a failure, your self-esteem lower than sea level. So be gentle to yourself. Allow yourself the following:

- Occasionally you'll feel upset even in the later stages of Emotional Rescue. Don't beat yourself up over this. Have a little down time where you don't make demands on yourself to be moving forward continually.

- Sometimes you'll get moody. You may miss your ex or have lots of regrets. These are OK as long as they remain the lesser portion of your day.

- You may make some silly decisions while you're finding your feet. Big deal! We all do! Again, don't beat yourself up about these. Learn from them and then leave them behind.

- You're allowed to be grumpy when you hear your ex is having fun! You're not a saint – you can only try your hardest not to let it get you down.

Your future

I'd like you to turn back to Chapter Three and page 48 to look at Your Essential Life Areas pyramid (ELA pyramid). As you're farther along in your stages of Emotional Rescue at this point I'd now like you to list one goal for each ELA you listed in Chapter 3.

Life Area: _____ New Goal: _____
Life Area: _____ New Goal: _____
Life Area: _____ New Goal: _____
Life Area: _____ New Goal: _____
Life Area: _____ New Goal: _____

One of the greatest things about the break-up of a major relationship (and *believe* me, you may not think there's anything great in it right now, but you'll be surprised later on) is that sometimes it leads you to an entirely new life – new career, new attitude to friends, family and children (if you have them), new interests and of course new loves. So this exercise is important to refocus you on the grand scheme of things – not just finding a new partner!

Common pitfalls to avoid

I know we weren't going to talk about your ex but I think you need to be aware of the following things. Particularly if you were the one left behind by your ex (that is, the dumpee), there are certain things to watch out for. You can stop yourself, with this awareness, from being stuck in old behaviour patterns.

- You find yourself while shopping, stocking up with your ex's favourite groceries/drinks.
- You can't quite bring yourself to throw away your ex's toothbrush that's rotting at the top of the bathroom cabinet.
- You find yourself lingering at the perfume/aftershave section of a store, smelling the scent your ex wore.
- You name your new pet goldfish, kitten or puppy after your ex.
- You catch yourself fixing the Sunday roast the way he/she loved even though it's a hassle.
- You find yourself having nightmares about him/her too frequently.
- You secretly hope mutual friends will mention news of your ex.
- You find yourself buying your ex's favourite video and watching it over and over, focussing on his/her favourite scenes.

These things mean that at a subconscious level you're not moving forward as much as you'd like to think. You still may have some bad habits to break in terms of your ex! But that's only natural. As well as all you've already learned about your break-up you'll continue to build on this. You'll come across new ways of dealing with memories of your ex (e.g. you may try all the tricks in the chapters of *The Break-Up Survival Kit* but then buy one of those voodoo dolls and pins and gleefully stick the pins in the doll. Or you end up creating your own secret 'spell' to ward off painful memories – different strokes for different folks!). You'll suddenly see things in a different light. The process of breaking up is a developing one. The best you can do is come out of it knowing more of what you want out of relationships and of what you don't want! And this has lots to do with how you see yourself and what you're now learning that you can obtain.

The R.E.S.C.U.E. Code

Here's a little something for you to remember when you're feeling doubtful or anxious. This should become your code for life so commit it to your memory.

R – Ready for anything. The new independent you will open your eyes to different experiences.

E – Expectations. You'll now have recovered enough emotionally to evaluate your expectations in terms of your life, loves and everything.

S – Seize moments. Even accepting the smallest invitation made out of the blue, such as having coffee with a work colleague can lift your spirits. I've never had anyone complain to me about the moments they've seized. But I've certainly had many express regret to me about those they didn't!

C – Care for yourself. Be aware of your low points. Be on guard against slipping back to any old romantic habits. Be alert to anyone trying to play on vulnerabilities you may still have from your break-up. For example, they may be simply lusting after you and know that you're a bit lonely!

U – Uplifting moments. These get more frequent as you travel along the new road your life has become.

E – Elation. One day elation will be yours when you've finally left your ex behind! Elation, if they weren't good to you – and now you

can see that! Elation, if you were hard on yourself after the break-up
– and now you aren't!

**The most important thing I've learned from this chapter about
moving on is:** _____
_____

And I'm going to remind myself of this.

Good luck and best wishes to all of you!